THE PRINCE

DISCOVER OUR BOOKS
ACCESSING HERE!

Copyright of this translation © IBC - Instituto Brasileiro De Cultura, 2023

Original title: The Prince
All rights reserved for this translation and production, by law 9.610 of 2.19.1998.

President: Paulo Roberto Houch
MTB 0083982/SP

Editorial Coordination: Paola Houch
Art Coordination: Rubens Martim (cover)
Translation: Francine Cervato
English text review: Francine Oliveira
Text Preparation: Fabio Kataoka
Review: Valéria Paixão e Rogério Coelho
Layout: Rogério Pires

Sales: Phone: +55 (11) 3393-7727 (comercial2@editoraonline.com.br)

The legal deposit was made.

Printed by PlenaPrint.
1st Print 2025

International Data of Cataloging in Publication (CIP) according to ISBD	
C181p	Camelot Editora
	The Prince / Camelot Editora. – Barueri : Camelot Editora, 2024. 96 p. ; 15,1cm x 23cm. Translation of: O Príncipe
	ISBN: 978-65-6095-102-0
	1. Political science. I. Title.
2024-1268	CDD 320 CDU 32
Elaborated by Vagner Rodolfo da Silva - CRB-8/9410	

IBC — Instituto Brasileiro de Cultura LTDA
CNPJ 04.207.648/0001-94
Avenida Juruá, 762 — Alphaville Industrial
ZIP CODE: 06455-010 — Barueri/SP
www.editoraonline.com.br

Niccolò Machiavelli
THE PRINCE

SUMMARY

NICCOLÒ MACHIAVELLI TO THE MAGNIFICENT LORENZO DE MEDICI..9

CHAPTER I..11
How many types of principalities are there, and by what means are they acquired
(Quot sint genera principatuum et quibus modis acquirantur)

CHAPTER II...11
Concerning hereditary principalities
(De principatibus hereditariis)

CHAPTER III..12
Concerning mixed principalities
(De principatibus mixtis)

CHAPTER IV..19
Why did the kingdom of Darius, conquered by Alexander, not rebel against the successors of Alexander at his death?
(Cur Darii regnum quod Alexander occupaverat a successoribus suis post Alexandri mortem non defecit)

CHAPTER V 22
Concerning the way to govern cities or principalities which lived under their own laws before they were annexed
(Quomodo administrandae sunt civitates vel principatus, qui antequam occuparentur, suis legibus vivebant)

CHAPTER VI..23
Concerning new principalities which are acquired by one's own weapons and virtue
(De principatibus novis qui armis propriis et virtute acquiruntur)

CHAPTER VII 26
Concerning new principalities which are acquired either by the weapons of others or by good fortune
(De principatibus novis qui alienis armis et fortuna acquiruntur)

CHAPTER VIII 32
Concerning those who obtained a principality by treacherous means
(De his qui per scelera ad principatum pervenere)

CHAPTER IX 36
Concerning a civil principality
(De principatu civili)

CHAPTER X 39
How should the strength of all principalities be measured?
(Quomodo omnium principatuum vires perpendi debeant)

CHAPTER XI 41
Concerning ecclesiastical principalities
(De principatibus eclesiasticis)

CHAPTER XII 43
How many kinds of militias are there? And concerning mercenaries
(Quot sint genera militiae et de mercenariis militibus)

CHAPTER XIII 47
Concerning auxiliaries, mixed and own soldiers
(De militibus auxiliariis, mixtis et propriis)

CHAPTER XIV 51
What concerns a prince about the militia?
(Quod principem deceat circa militiam)

CHAPTER XV 53
Concerning things for which men, and especially princes, are praised or blamed
(De his rebus quibus homines, et praesertim principes, laudantur aut vituperantur)

CHAPTER XVI 55
Concerning liberality and parsimony
(De liberalitate et parsimonia)

CHAPTER XVII 57
Cruelty and mercy, and whether it is better to be loved than feared, or rather feared than loved
(De crudelitate et pietate; et an sit melius amari quam timeri, vel e contra)

CHAPTER XVIII 60
In what way should princes keep faith in the word given?
(*Quomodo fides a principibus sit servanda*)

CHAPTER XIX 62
How to avoid being despised and hated
(*De contemptu et odio fugiendo*)

CHAPTER XX 71
Whether fortresses and many other things made by princes are useful or not
(*An arces et multa alia quae cotidie a principibus fiunt utilia an inutilia sint*)

CHAPTER XXI 75
What is appropriate to a prince to be esteemed
(*Quod principem deceat ut egregius habeatur*)

CHAPTER XXII 78
Concerning the secretaries that princes have with them
(*De his quos a secretis principes habent*)

CHAPTER XXIII 79
How flatterers should be avoided
(*Quomodo adulatores sint fugiendi*)

CHAPTER XXIV 81
Why did the princes of Italy lose their states?
(*Cur Italiae principes regnum amiserunt*)

CHAPTER XXV 83
How much can fortune affect human affairs, and how can it be withstood?
(*Quantum fortuna in rebus humanis possit, et quomodo illi sit occurren dum*)

CHAPTER XXVI 86
An exhortation to take Italy and free it from the hands of the barbarians
(*Exhortatio ad capessendam italiam in libertatemque a barbaris vindicandam*)

LETTER TO FRANCESCO VETTORI 90

Statue of Machiavelli in the Galleria Degli Uffizi, Florence.

THE PRINCE

Niccolò Machiavelli to the magnificent Lorenzo de Medici

Those who strive to obtain the good graces of a prince usually offer him the rarest thing they have or what they think is most to his liking; hence one often sees horses, weapons, brocades, precious stones, and other ornaments being offered to him, worthy of his greatness.

Wanting, therefore, to present myself with some testimony that proves my admiration for your Magnificence, I did not find among my possessions anything of greater value or that I value as much as the knowledge of the actions of great men, acquired by long experience of modern things, and in a continuous lesson of the ancient ones, which, having meditated on for a long time and examined with great diligence, I have now brought together in the small volume that I send to your Magnificence. And, although I may consider this work unworthy of being offered to you, I trust, however, that you will receive it, considering that I cannot offer you a better gift than to facilitate for you, in a very short time, what took me many years, and with so many troubles and dangers.

I did not embellish the work with brilliant and pompous words, nor with any of those vain ornaments with which many authors are accustomed to embellishing and describing their works; for I only wanted, either that nothing honors it or that only the variety of the matter and the gravity of the matter make it acceptable. Nor do I want it to be considered presumptuous that a man from a low and insignificant state dares to discuss and give rules about the concerns of princes; because, just as those who draw landscapes place themselves on the plains to consider the nature of mountains and hills, and, to consider the plains, they place themselves on top of the mountains, in the same way, to know well the nature of people, it is necessary to be a prince, and to understand the nature of princes it is necessary to be a son of the people.

May Your Magnificence accept this small gift with the enthusiasm in which I send it to you, and if you read it and meditate on it carefully, you will find within it the burning desire that I have for you to reach the greatness that fortune and your other qualities promise you. And if, from the top of your height, you turn your eyes to these low places, you will recognize how unworthily I endure a great and continuous adversity of fortune.

"The natural prince has fewer reasons and less need to offend."

CHAPTER I
How many types of principalities are there, and by what means are they acquired
(Quot sint genera principatuum et quibus modis acquirantur)

All states, all governments that had and have empired over men, were and are either republics or principalities. Principalities are either hereditary, because their ancestors were princes by blood and for a long time, or they are new. The new ones are either entirely new, like Milan for Francisco Sforza, or they are new as added members to the hereditary state of the prince who annexes them, like the kingdom of Naples for the king of Spain. These domains thus conquered are either used to live under the tutelage of a prince, or enjoy its freedom, and are conquered with other people's weapons or with their own, by fortune or merit.

CHAPTER II
Concerning hereditary principalities
(De principatibus hereditariis)

I will not deal with republics at this point; I will focus only on principalities. I will outline the principles described and discuss how they should be ruled and maintained. I say, therefore, that for the preservation of hereditary states and being fond of the lineage of their prince, the difficulties are much less than in the new ones, as it is enough not to neglect the customs of the ancestors and, later, to temporize with fortuitous events, so that, if such a prince is endowed with ordinary capacity, he will always remain in power, unless an extraordinary and excessive force deprives him of it. Once removed from power, even if the usurper is fearsome, he regains power.

We have in Italy, for example, the Duke of Ferrara, who did not give in to the assaults of the Venetians in 1484 nor to those of Pope Julius in 1510, simply because he was long-established in that domain. In fact, the natural prince has fewer reasons and less need to offend. We then conclude that he should be more loved, and if he is not hated due to uncontrolled vices, it is logical and natural that he should be liked by everyone. And in antiquity and the continuation of the exercise of power, the memories and causes of innovations are erased, because a change always lays the foundation for the construction of another one.

CHAPTER III
Concerning mixed principalities
(De principatibus mixtis)

However, it is in the new principalities that the difficulties occur. Firstly, if it is not entirely new, it is a member annexed to a hereditary state (which, as a whole, can be considered almost mixed), its variations resulting mainly from a natural difficulty inherent to all new principalities: it is that men, with satisfaction, change rulers thinking about improving, and this belief makes them take up weapons against their current ruler. They are deceived because, from their own experience, they later realize that they have made the situation worse. This depends on another natural and ordinary necessity, which causes that the new prince always needs to offend the new subjects with his soldiers and with other infinite insults that are thrown at the recent conquest. In this way, you have as enemies all those you offended with the occupation of that principality, and you cannot keep as friends those who placed you there, because you cannot satisfy them in the way they had imagined, nor apply violent correctives to them once you are obliged to them; because always, even if very strong in armies, the support of the inhabitants is needed to penetrate a province. It was for these reasons that Louis XII, king of France, quickly occupied Milan and then lost it. Initially, Ludovico's forces were enough, because those populations that had opened their doors to him, recognizing the mistake of their previous thinking, and disbelievers in the future well-being they had imagined, could no longer bear the unpleasantness caused by the new prince.

It is known that, when reconquering the rebellious regions, they hardly lose them. The ruler, due to the rebellion, is less hesitant to ensure the punishment of those who failed him with loyalty, to investigate the suspects, and to repair the weakest points. Thus, to cause France to lose Milan the first time, it was enough for Duke Ludovico to raise insurrections on the borders; but to cause him to lose it a second time, it was necessary to bring the whole world against him, and that his armies were defeated and expelled from Italy, which resulted from the reasons mentioned above. Nevertheless, Milan was taken from France both the first and second times.

Let's now talk about the second time and see what resources France had at its disposal and what means anyone who finds themselves in such a situation could use in order to better keep the conquest.

These states conquered and annexed to an ancient state are either of the same province and of the same language, or they are not. When they are, it is generally easy to keep them submissive, especially when they are not used to living in freedom; and to dominate them, it will surely be enough to have extinguished the lineage of the prince who governed them, because regarding other things, when you preserve their old conditions and there are not changes in customs, men begin to live peacefully, as we saw in Burgundy, Brittany, Gascony, and Normandy, that were bound to France for so long: despite the relative difference in languages, but thanks to the similarity of customs, they easily adapted between them. And whoever conquers, wanting to preserve them, must adopt two measures: the first, make the lineage of the former prince extinct; the other, not changing either its laws or taxes; in such a way that, in a very short period of time, the conquered territory starts to form a whole body with the old principality.

When territories are conquered in a province with a different language, customs, and laws, difficulties begin to arise, and it takes a lot of good fortune and skill to keep them. And one of the greatest and most efficient resources would be one of the conquerors to go and inhabit there. This would make the acquired possession safer and more lasting, as happened with the Turk in Greece, who, despite having observed all local laws, would not have kept this territory if he had not moved there. This is because, being on-site, it is possible to see riots arise, and they can be repressed. Not being on site, one only hears about them when the confusion is already widespread and no longer capable of being solved. In addition, the conquered province is not plundered by the temporary administrators that occupy it. The subjects are satisfied because resources to the prince become easier. Thus, they have more reasons to love him, wanting to be good, and to fear him if they want to act differently. Whoever from abroad wishes to attack that state will have greater respect for it; by inhabiting it, the prince will only lose it with great difficulty.

Another efficient way is to install colonies in one or two points that are chained to that state, or keep many troops there. Colonies can be installed and maintained without much cost. Its creation harms only those whose fields and houses are taken away and given to the new inhabitants, who constitute a minimum portion of the conquered state. Those who are harmed, remaining dispersed and poor, cannot cause any harm, while those who are not harmed remain aside, frightened, and must calm down the thought that they cannot make mistakes so that the same thing does not happen to them as happened to those that were despoiled.

Therefore, colonies are not onerous; they are more faithful, they offend less; and those that are harmed cannot cause harm, becoming poor and dispersed, as has already been said. Hence, it follows that men must be cherished or eliminated because, if they take revenge for small offenses, they cannot do so for serious ones; hence, it follows that the offense done to man must be such that revenge cannot be feared. But by maintaining military forces instead of colonies much more is spent, absorbing all the revenue of that state in the guard deployed there; in this way, the conquest becomes a loss and offends much more because it damages the entire country with changes in the army's accommodation, an inconvenience that everyone feels and that turns each inhabitant into an enemy, and it is enemies that can cause harm to the conqueror, even if defeated in their own home. From any point of view, this armed guard is useless, while the creation of colonies is useful.

Whoever is at the head of a different province must become the leader and defender of his less powerful neighbors, weaken the more powerful amongst them, and take care that under no circumstances an outsider as strong as him can penetrate there. And there will always be someone called upon by those who feel discontent in the province, whether due to excessive ambition or fear, as did the Aetolians who incorporated the Romans into Greece, and who, in fact, in all the other provinces they conquered, were helped by the respective inhabitants.

When a powerful foreigner penetrates a province, all those who are weaker will join him, moved by envy against those who have become powerful over them. So much so that, regarding these, it is not necessary to do much work to obtain their support, as all of them, soon, voluntarily, form a block with their conquered state. Care must be taken not to allow them to assume too much power and authority. The conqueror can easily, with its forces and their support, slaughter those that are still strong, to become the absolute master of that province. And whoever does not satisfactorily carry out this part will soon lose its achievement, and, as long as it can be kept, it will experience countless annoyances and difficulties.

The Romans, in the provinces which they annexed, observed closely these points: they founded colonies, won the friendship of the less influential without increasing their power, slaughtered the strongest, and did not let powerful foreigners acquire prestige. I take only the province of Greece as an example. The Achaeans and Aetolians became friends with the Romans. The kingdom of the Macedonians was slaughtered, and Antiochus was driven out from there, but not even the merits of the Achaeans and Aetolians assured them permission to conquer any state. Neither Philip's persuasion managed to make the Romans become his allies and not diminish him, nor did Antiochus' power manage to make them authorize him to maintain his domain in that province. This all occurred because the Romans did in these cases what every intelligent prince must do: not only watch and be careful with present troubles, but also with future ones, avoiding them with all caution because, if foreseen in time, it is easy to remedy them; but, waiting for them to approach, the medicine does not arrive in time, and the malady has already become incurable. It happens here as in the case of tuberculosis, according to physicians: in the beginning, it is easy to cure and difficult to detect. However, over time, if the disease is not known or treated, it becomes easy to detect and difficult to cure. This also occurs in the affairs of the state because, knowing in advance the evils that affect it (which are only given to a wise man to see), the cure is quick; but when, because they were not immediately known, they grow in a way that everyone can see them, there is no longer any remedy.

The Romans, foreseeing the disturbances, always hindered wars, never to escape them, but to allow them to take their course, as they knew that war cannot be avoided, only postponed for the benefit of others. That is why they promoted war against Philip and Antiochus in Greece. It was to avoid having to do it in Italy, and, however, they could have avoided the fight at that time if they wanted to. Nor, at any time, did they like what was on the lips of the experts of our time every day, the wish to enjoy the benefits of our time, but rather only what resulted from their own virtue and prudence: in truth, time casts all the things ahead and can turn good into evil and evil into good.

Let us go back to France and analyze whether it did any of the things mentioned; I am talking about Louis and not about Charles, as he was the one who, by having maintained the longest rule in Italy, the progress was best seen, and you will see that he did the opposite of what must be done to maintain a state in a different province.

King Louis was taken to Italy by the ambition of the Venetians, who, by this means, wanted to gain the state of Lombardy. I do not wish to censure the course taken by the king because, wanting to start setting foot in Italy and having no friends in this province, all doors closed due to King Charles' behavior, and he was forced to make use of those friendships which he could count on, and he would have succeeded if, in other matters, he had not made some mistakes. Once Lombardy was conquered, the king promptly reacquired the reputation that Charles had lost: Genoa gave in; the Florentines became his friends; the Marquis of Mantua, the

Duke of Ferrara, Bentivoglio, the lady of Forli, the lord of Faenza, of Pesaro, of Rimini, of Camerino, of Piombino, the Lucchese, the Pisans, and the Sienese, all of them went to meet him to become his friends. The Venetians were then able to consider the temerity of the resolution they had adopted, since, in order to conquer two towns in Lombardy, they made the king master of two thirds of Italy.

How easily the king could have maintained his reputation in Italy if, observing the rules already mentioned, he had kept safe and defended all those of his friends that, although in large numbers, were weak and fearful, some afraid of the Church, some of the Venetians, and thus they would always have been forced to stand in with him, and by their means, he could easily have made himself secure against those who remained powerful.

However, having just arrived in Milan, he did the opposite, helping Pope Alexander occupy Romagna. He did not even realize that with this deliberation he was weakening himself, depriving himself of friends and those who had thrown themselves into his arms, while he was magnifying the Church by adding to the spiritual power, which gives him so much authority, such temporal power. Having made his first mistake, he was compelled to continue making others until, to put an end to Alexander's ambition and prevent him from becoming master of Tuscany, he had to go to Italy in person. It was not enough for him to have made the Church great and deprived himself of his friends. Because he wanted the kingdom of Naples, he divided it with the king of Spain; being the prime arbiter in Italy, he placed an associate there so that the ambitious ones of that province and those dissatisfied with him would have someone to turn, and instead of leaving a sovereign subject to him in that kingdom, he removed him to, in his place, put someone else who could drive him from there.

The wish to conquer is very natural and common, and whenever men can do so, they will be praised or, at least, they will not be blamed; but when they have no possibility and want to do it anyway, here is the mistake and, consequently, the blame. If France, then, could assault Naples with its forces, it should do so; if it could not, it should not divide this kingdom. And if the division it made with the Venetians over Lombardy was justified by the excuse that, by it, a foothold in Italy was established, that one deserves blame because it is not justified by this need.

King Louis made these five mistakes: he eliminated the minor powers; he increased the strength of one of the greater powers in Italy; there he placed a very powerful foreigner; he did not come to live in the country and did not install colonies.

However, these mistakes could not have caused harm while he lived, if he had not made the sixth mistake of taking the territories from the Venetians. In fact, if he had not aggrandized the Church nor introduced Spain into Italy, it would have been quite reasonable and necessary to weaken them, but having first taken these steps, they should never have consented to their ruin. This is because, being powerful, they would have always kept those at a distance from Lombardy, as the Venetians would never consent to any maneuver against that state, unless they became the masters, in the same way that the others would not want to take it over from France to give it to the Venetians, at the same time that they lacked the courage to fight with them and with France. And if someone said: King Louis yielded Romagna to Alexander and the kingdom to Spain to avoid a war, I would answer with the reasons previously stated that a crisis should never be allowed to continue to escape a war, even because it is not to be avoided, but it is only postponed to one's own disadvantage. And if some others alleged the promise that the king had made to the pope to carry out that conquest for him in exchange for the dissolution of his marriage and the cardinal's hat for the archbishop of Rouen, I would answer with what will be said later about the word of princes and how to respect it.

King Louis lost Lombardy for not having respected any of the principles observed by others who dominated provinces and wanted to keep them. There is no miracle here, but it is very common and reasonable. And I spoke of this matter in Nantes to the Archbishop of Rouen, when Valentino, popularly called Cesare Borgia, the son of Pope Alexander, occupied Romagna. Because, when the Cardinal of Rouen told me that the Italians did not understand war, I replied that the French did not understand the state; if they did, they would not have allowed the

Church to achieve such greatness. From experience, it was seen that the greatness of the Church and of Spain in Italy was caused by France, and its ruin may be attributed to them. From this, we derive a general rule that never or rarely fails: whoever is the cause of someone's power is ruined, because this power results either from cunning or from force, and both are suspects for the one who became powerful.

CHAPTER IV
WHY DID THE KINGDOM OF DARIUS, CONQUERED BY ALEXANDER, NOT REBEL AGAINST THE SUCCESSORS OF ALEXANDER AT HIS DEATH?

(Cur Darii regnum quod Alexander occupaverat a successoribus suis post Alexandri mortem non defecit)

Considering the difficulties that need to be faced to preserve a newly conquered state, one could be appalled by the fact that, having become master of Asia in a few years, not only had his occupation ended, Alexander the Great died, and, despite it seeming reasonable that the whole state should rebel, his successors maintained it and found no other difficulty than that which arose among themselves from their own ambitions. The justification is that the principalities that can be remembered have been governed in two different ways: either by a prince, with all the others being servants who, as ministers by his grace and permission, help to govern the state, or by a prince and barons, who, not by the grace of the prince but by the antiquity of blood, have that degree of ministers. These barons have their own states and subjects who recognize them as lords and have a natural affection for them. States that are governed by a prince and his servants have the one with greater authority, because throughout their province there is no one recognized as ruler other than him, and if the subjects obey someone else, they do so because of their position as minister and official, not giving him the slightest esteem.

The examples of these two types of government are, in our times, the Turk and that of the king of France. The whole monarchy of the Turk is governed by one lord; the others are his servants, and, dividing his kingdom into sanjaks, he has different administrators there, and changes them as he chooses. But the king of France is in the midst of a multitude of former lords that, in this capacity, are recognized by their subjects and loved by them; they have their pre-eminences, and the king cannot deprive them of these pre-eminences without danger to himself. Whoever sets its sights on one or another of these governments will find difficulties in conquering the state of the Turk, but, once it is conquered, there will be great ease in maintaining it; on the other hand, there will be in every sense greater ease in occupying the state of France, but great difficulty in maintaining it.

The causes of the difficulties in occupying the kingdom of the Turk are that the usurper cannot be called in by the princes of that kingdom, nor can he hope to be assisted in his undertaking by the uprising of those whom the lord has around him. This arises from the reasons given above. Because they are all slaves and bondmen, they are more difficult to corrupt, and when they are bribed, little use can be expected, since they are not capable of dragging the people behind them, for the reasons already mentioned. Therefore, if someone attacks the state of the Turk, it must bear in mind that it will find it united, and it is advisable to rely more on its own forces than on the uprising of others. But, once conquered and defeated in a pitched battle so that he cannot rebuild his armies, there is nothing to fear other than the prince's dynasty; once this is extinct, no one is left who should be feared, since the others do not enjoy prestige among the people; and as the winner of this could not expect anything before victory, after it, he must not fear it.

The opposite occurs in kingdoms like France because one can easily invade there by gaining over some barons of the kingdom, as they are always discontented and eager for innovations. These, for the reasons mentioned, can open access to that state and facilitate victory. But if you wish to maintain it, it will bring countless difficulties, whether with those who helped you or with those you oppressed. It is not enough to extinguish the prince's lineage, as there remain those lords who become leaders of the new revolutions, and, being unable neither to satisfy them nor to exterminate them, that state is lost whenever time brings the opportunity.

Now, if you consider what the nature of the government of Darius was, you will find it similar to the kingdom of the Turk. For Alexander, it was first necessary to corner him and defeat him in a pitched battle, and after the victory, with Darius dead, that state became safe for Alexander for the reasons explained. His successors, if they had been united, could have enjoyed it peacefully, as no other turmoil arose there other than that caused by themselves.

As for organized states like France, it is impossible to possess them with such tranquility. It was from this circumstance that the frequent rebellions of Spain, France, and Greece against the Romans arose. Due to the large number of principalities that existed in those states and as long as the memory of them endured, the Romans were insecure in their possession of those domains. But with the memory of principalities extinguished and with the power and constancy of their authority, the Romans became secure rulers. They were also able, later fighting in internal struggles, to drag each faction to their side, part of those provinces, according to the authority they had acquired with them; and these provinces, as the blood of their former lords no longer existed, recognized only the sovereignty of the Romans. Therefore, considering all these things, no one will marvel at the ease that Alexander found in preserving the State of Asia and the difficulties that others had in maintaining what was conquered, such as Pyrrhus and many others. This did not result from the great or little virtue of the conqueror, but rather from the diversity of form of the object of conquest.

CHAPTER V
Concerning the Way to Govern Cities or Principalities Which Lived Under Their Own Laws Before They Were Annexed

(Quomodo administrandae sunt civitates vel principatus, qui antequam occuparentur, suis legibus vivebant)

As it was said, when those states that are conquered are accustomed to living under their own laws and in freedom, there are three ways to preserve them: the first is to ruin them; the next is to go and inhabit them in person; and the third is to let them live with their laws, collecting tribute and creating within them a government of a few who remain friends, because, as this government was created by that prince, it knows that it cannot remain without his friendship and power, and everything to preserve them must be done. Wanting to preserve a city accustomed to living freely, is easier than any other way to preserve it through its citizens.

Let's remember the Spartans and the Romans. The Spartans took Athens and Thebes, creating a government of a few; however, they lost them. The Romans, to preserve Capua, Carthage, and Numantia, destroyed them and did not lose them. They wanted to preserve Greece almost as the Spartans did, making it free and leaving it with its own laws, but they were unable to do so. As a result, to preserve it, they were forced to destroy many cities in that province.

The truth is, there is no safe way to preserve such conquests other than destruction. And whoever becomes master of a city accustomed to living free and does not destroy it, expects to be destroyed by it, because it always finds, to support its rebellion, the name of freedom and that of its ancient institutions, never forgotten neither by the passage of time nor by the benefits received. No matter how much is done and provided for, if the inhabitants do not dissolve or disintegrate; they do not forget that name or those institutions, and then, at every incident, they resort to them, as Pisa did a hundred years after being subjected to the Florentines.

However, when cities or provinces are accustomed to living under a prince and the dynasty is extinct, on the one hand, they are accustomed to obeying and, on the other hand, they do not have the former prince, they hardly reach an agreement to choose another prince; they do not know, anyway, how to live in freedom. In this way, they are slower to take up weapons, and, more easily, a prince can defeat them and take possession of them. However, in republics, there is more life, more hatred, and more desire for revenge; they do not and cannot allow the memory of ancient freedom to fade; therefore, the safest way is to destroy them or inhabit them in person.

CHAPTER VI
Concerning new principalities which are acquired by one's own weapons and virtue

(De principatibus novis qui armis propriis et virtute acquiruntur)

Regarding entirely new principalities, I would like to talk about prince and state. I will point out examples of great characters; because men walk almost always on paths beaten by others, proceeding in their actions by imitations, and it is not possible to faithfully follow other people's paths or achieve the virtue of what they imitate, a wise man must always follow the paths taken by those who have become great and imitate those who have been excellent. This is so that, if it is not possible to reach their virtue, at least he will benefit from it. Let him act like the clever archers that, considering the point they want to reach very far away and knowing how far the capacity of their bow goes, aim much higher than the target location, not to reach as high a height with their arrow, but to be able, with the aid of such a high aim, to reach their target.

Thus, I say that in an entirely new principality, where there is a new prince, there is more or less difficulty in maintaining it, depending on whether it is more or less virtuous that who conquers the state. And because rising from private to prince presupposes either virtue or fortune, it seems that one or other of these two reasons will mitigate to some degree many difficulties; nevertheless, it has been observed that the one that relied the least on fortune retained power most securely. Further, it facilitates matters when the prince, having no other state, is compelled to inhabit it in person.

To mention those who, by their own virtue and not by fortune, became princes, I say that the greatest are Moses, Cyrus, Romulus, Theseus, and others. Although Moses should not be considered because he was a mere executor of the will of God, however, he should be admired only for the grace that made him worthy to speak with God. But let's consider Cyrus and the others who conquered or founded kingdoms, all admirable. And if their particular actions and orders are considered, these will appear to be no different from those of Moses, who had such a great preceptor. And examining their actions and lives, it is not seen that they had anything of fortune other than the occasion, which provided them with the means to adapt things in the way that best suited them; and, without that opportunity, their personal value would have been erased, and without that virtue, the opportunity would have come in vain.

Moses needed to find the people of Israel in Egypt, enslaved and oppressed by the Egyptians, so that they, in order to free themselves from slavery, would be willing to follow him. It was necessary that Romulus could not be kept in Alba, and was exposed at birth so that he could become king of Rome and founder of that fatherland. It was necessary for Cyrus to find the Persians who were discontented with the Medes' empire, and these were softened and fragile by the prolonged peace. Theseus could not demonstrate his virtue if the Athenians were not dispersed. Therefore, these opportunities made these men happy, and their excellent ability made that occasion known to each one. As a result, their fatherland was ennobled, and became very happy.

Those who, by their virtues, similar to those they had, become princes, conquer the principality with difficulty but easily maintain it, and the obstacles that are presented to them when conquering the principality in part arise from the new arrangements and systems of government that they are forced to introduce to found their state and establish its security.

It must be considered that there is nothing more difficult to take care of, more doubtful to achieve, or more dangerous to handle, than becoming a leader and introducing new orders. This is because the introducer has as enemies all those who obtained advantages from the old institutions and finds weak defenders in those who benefit from the new orders. This weakness arises partly from the fear of the opponents that still have the laws to serve their interests, and partly from the incredulity of men: these, in truth, do not believe in innovations if they do not see them as the result of firm experience. Thus, it happens that any time the enemies have the opportunity to attack, they do so with sectarian heat, while the others defend weakly so that alongside them there is a serious danger.

To explain this part well, it is necessary to analyze whether these innovators can rely on themselves or have to depend on others, that is, whether to carry out their work they need to pray or whether they can actually use force. In the first case, they always end badly and achieve nothing; but when they depend on themselves and use force, then they are rarely in danger. Hence, all the armed prophets won, and the unarmed ones failed. Because, in addition to the facts mentioned, the nature of people is varied, making it easy to persuade them of one thing, but difficult to fix them in that persuasion. It is therefore important to be prepared so that, when they no longer believe, it may be possible to make them believe by force.

Moses, Cyrus, Theseus, and Romulus would not have been able to maintain their constitutions for a long time if they were unarmed; as happened in our times to Friar Girolamo Savonarola, who failed in his new order of things when the crowd started disbelieving in him, and he had no means to keep steadfast those who believed, nor to make the unbelievers come to believe. Therefore, people in this situation have great difficulties conducting themselves, and all dangers will be in their path. It is important that they overcome them with courage, but when these are overcome, they begin to be venerated, except for those who were jealous of their condition; the brave become powerful, safe, honored, and happy.

To these great examples, I wish to add a lesser one, which will have some resemblance to them and which I think is enough for all others similar: the Hiero of Syracuse. This one, in particular, became prince of Syracuse; he also owed nothing to fortune, but opportunity, because, when the Syracusans were oppressed, they chose him for their captain; afterward, he became prince. And he was of such virtue, even in his private life, that the one who wrote about him said: *quod nihil illi deerat ad regnandum praeter regnum* (that he needed nothing but a kingdom to be a king).

He extinguished the old militia, organized the new one, abandoned old alliances, made new ones; and, as he had his own allies and soldiers, he was able, on such foundations, to build the works he wanted – so much so that it took him a lot of effort to conquer and little to maintain.

CHAPTER VII
Concerning new principalities which are acquired either by the weapons of others or by good fortune

(De principatibus novis qui alienis armis et fortuna acquiruntur)

Those who became princes only due to their fortune rose with little effort, but only with a lot of effort. They remain that way: they have no difficulties on the way up because they fly, but all sorts of difficulties arise after they are there. They are those to whom a state is granted, whether for money or by grace of the grantor: as happened to many in Greece, in the cities of Ionia and Hellespont, where princes were made by Darius in order that they might preserve the cities both for his security and his glory; as were also made those emperors who, by the corruption of the soldiers, from private individuals, achieved domain of the Empire.

These are simply subject to the will and fortune of those who granted them the state, which are two highly fickle and unstable things: and they do not know and cannot maintain their position. They do not know because, if they are not men of great worth and virtue, it is not reasonable that, having always lived in a private environment, they know how to command; they cannot because they do not have forces that they can keep friendly and faithful. Furthermore, states that emerge quickly, like all other things in nature that are born and grow quickly, cannot have perfect roots and structures, so that the first adversity extinguishes them. Unless those who, as it was said, suddenly become princes, are men of such virtue that they immediately know how to prepare themselves to preserve what fortune placed in their laps, subsequently forming the foundations that the others established before they became princes.

Concerning these two ways of becoming a prince, by virtue or by fortune, I point out two examples that occurred in the days of our memory: these are Francesco Sforza and Cesare Borgia. Francesco, by proper means and with great virtue, from being a private person became Duke of Milan; and what with a thousand efforts he had achieved, with little effort he maintained.

Cesare Borgia, called by the people Duke Valentino, acquired his state during the ascendancy of his father, and on its decline, he lost it. This, despite the fact that he used all the means and did everything that should be done by a wise and virtuous man, took root in those states that the weapons and fortune of others had granted him. Because, as it was said previously, the one who does not lay the foundations first will only be able to establish them later with great virtue, even if this is done with trouble for the builder and danger for the building. If it is considered all the progress made by the duke, it will be seen that he laid great foundations for his future power, and I do not think it superfluous to describe them, because I do not know what better precepts to give a new prince than the example of his actions; and if his dispositions did not benefit him, it was not his fault, but rather as a result of extraordinary and extreme malignity of fortune.

Alexander VI, in wanting to aggrandize his son, the duke, had many present and future difficulties. First, he saw no way of being able to make him master of any state that was not a state of the Church, and if he was willing to take one of these, he knew that the Duke of Milan and the Venetians would not allow it because Faenza and Rimini were already under the protection of the Venetians. Furthermore, he saw that the weapons of Italy, and especially those that could be used, were in the hands of those who should fear the greatness of the pope; he could not trust them, therefore, as all of them belonged to the Orsini and Colonna and their supporters. It was necessary to disturb the organization of the Italian states and disarticulate those belonging to them, in order to be able to securely master part of them. This was easy for him to do, as he found the Venetians, moved by other reasons, inclined to bring back the French into Italy, which he not only did not oppose but also made it easier with the dissolution of King Louis' first marriage. Therefore, the king went to Italy with the help of the Venetians and the consent of Alexander. He was no sooner in Milan, when the pope obtained troops for the conquest of Romagna, which became possible due to the king's reputation.

After occupying Romagna and defeating the supporters of Colonna, the duke intended to maintain the conquest and advance further. Two things prevented him: one, the troops that did not seem faithful to him; the other, the will of France; that is, the duke feared that the troops of Orsini, which he had made use of, would fail to him, not only preventing him from conquering but also taking from him what he conquered, as well as fearing that the king might also do the same. Of the Orsini, he had proof when, after taking Faenza and attacking Bologna, he saw them coldly carry out this attack; concerning the king, he knew his disposition when, having taken the duchy of Urbino, he attacked Tuscany; the king made him give up this campaign.

Consequently, the duke decided to no longer depend on the weapons and fortunes of others. Initially, he weakened the Orsini and Colonna factions in Rome. To this end, he attracted to himself all their followers who were gentlemen, making them his gentlemen and giving them wealth and honor. According to their qualities, with commands and governments, so that, in a few months, the affection they maintained for the factions was extinguished and turned entirely to the duke. Then, he waited for the opportunity to eliminate the Orsini after dispersing the Colonna, an opportunity that came well to him and which he took advantage of. Because the Orsini had realized, too late, that the greatness of the duke and the Church was their ruin, they organized a conference in Magione, in Perugia. From this conference sprang the rebellion of Urbino, the riots in Romagna, and countless dangers for the duke, who overcame them all with the help of the French.

RHaving regained his reputation, not trusting France or other foreign troops so as not to have them strengthened, he resorted to cunning. And he knew so well how to conceal his feelings that the Orsini, by the mediation of Mr. Pagolo, reconciled with him: to better assure himself of this intermediary, the duke did not fail to provide him with courtesy of all kinds, giving him money, clothes, and horses; so that the simplicity of the Orsini led them to Senigallia, in the hands of the duke. Having eliminated these leaders, transforming their supporters into his friends, the duke had laid good foundations for his power, as he controlled all of Romagna and the duchy of Urbino, and even seemed to have become friends with Romagna and gained for himself all those populations that started experiencing the benefits of his government.

When the duke occupied Romagna, he found it under the rule of weak masters, who had plundered their subjects more quickly than they had ruled them, giving them cause for disunity instead of union, so that province was full of robberies, fights, and many other causes of insolence. The duke deemed it necessary to make it peaceful and obedient to the royal power and to give it a good government. That is why he promoted Ramiro d'Orco, a cruel and attentive man, to whom he gave the fullest powers. This man, in a short time, made it peaceful and united, with a great reputation.

Afterward, the duke understood that such excessive authority was not necessary, fearing that it would become hateful; he installed a civil court in the center of the province, with an excellent president, where each city had its own representative. And because he knew that the excesses of the past had given rise to some hatred, to cleanse the spirits of those populations and conquer them completely, he wanted to show that, if any cruelty had occurred, it was not born of him but rather of the sad and cruel nature of the minister. And, taking advantage of the opportunity, he had him placed, one morning, in the public square of Casena, cut into two pieces, with a stick and a bloody knife beside him. The ferocity of this spectacle made the population both satisfied and astonished.

The duke, finding himself quite strong and relatively assured against the present dangers, by having armed himself in his own way and having largely dispersed those troops that, in his vicinity, could injure him and wanting to continue with his conquest, was left with the fear of the king of France, because he knew how such a course would not be supported by him, who too late was aware of his mistake. And from this time on, he began to look for new alliances and turn his back on France in the incursion that the French made in the kingdom of Naples against the Spanish, who were besieging Gaeta. His intention was to secure himself against them, which would have had an immediate effect if Alexander had not died.

As to the present, this was his policy. But, as to future ones, he had to fear, initially, that a new successor to the government of the Church might not be friendly to him and would seek to take from him what Alexander had given him, and he thought of proceeding in four ways: first, to extinguish the families of those lords he had despoiled, to be able to deprive the pope of that opportunity; second, to conquer all the gentlemen of Rome, as it was said, in order to be able to keep the pope at bay with them; third, to make the college more to himself as possible; fourth, to conquer so much power before the pope died, that he could by himself withstand a first impact.

Of these four things, at the death of Alexander, he had accomplished three, the fourth being almost finished: because of the dispossessed lords, he had killed as many as he could reach, and very few had escaped; he had gained the support of the Roman gentlemen, and, in the college, he had great influence; and, as for the new conquest, he decided to become master of Tuscany – he already possessed Perugia and Piombino, and Pisa was under his protection.

As he no longer needed to respect France (which had belittled him because the French were already driven out of the kingdom by the Spanish, so each of them needed to buy his friendship), he invaded Pisa. After that, Lucca and Siena would readily give in, partly out of envy of the Florentines, partly out of fear; the Florentines had no one to turn to, which, if it had happened (it would have happened in the same year that Alexander died), would have given him so much power and reputation that he would have stood by himself, no longer depending on fortune and the forces of others, but rather on his own power and virtue. But Alexander died five years after he began to draw his sword. He left the duke with only the state of Romagna consolidated, with all the others in the air, in the midst of two very strong enemy armies, and sick to death.

There was so much indomitable bravery and virtue in the duke; he knew so well how men are conquered or lost, and the foundations he had laid in such a short time were completely solid that, if he had not had those armies upon him or if he had been in good health, he would have overcome any difficulty. And it is seen that his foundations were good, for the Romagna awaited him for more than a month. In Rome, although only half alive, he remained safe, and although the Baglioni, Vitelli, and Orsini came to Rome, they could do nothing against him. If he could not make the pope the one he wanted, at least he prevented the one he did not want from becoming pope. But if he had been healthy at the time of Alexander's death, everything would have been different for him. He told me, on the day that Pope Julius II was elected, that he had considered everything that could happen at the death of his father and had found a remedy for everything, but he had never thought, apart from his father's death, that he himself would be on the point to die.

Having exposed all the actions of the duke in this way, I would not know how to rebuke him; rather, I think that, as I did, I should be proposed for imitation to all those who, by fortune and with the weapons of others, rose to power. Because, having great spirit and high intention, he could not behave otherwise, and only the shortness of Alexander's life and his own sickness frustrated his designs. Therefore, the one who considers it necessary, in his new principality, to secure himself against enemies, to acquire friends, to win either by force or by fraud, to make himself beloved and feared by the people, to be followed and revered by the soldiers, to eliminate those who can or have reasons to offend, to order old institutions in new ways, to be severe and grateful, magnanimous and liberal, to extinguish the unfaithful militia, to create a new one, to maintain the friendship with kings and princes, so that they benefit with goodwill or offend with fear, cannot find more recent examples than the actions of the duke.

> *"If he could not make the pope the one he wanted, at least he prevented the one he did not want from becoming pope."*

He can only be blamed for the bad choice he made in electing Pope Julius to the pontificate, because, as it was said, not being able to elect a pope according to his wish, at least he prevented the one he did not want from becoming pope, and he should never consent to the election of any cardinal who had been offended by him, or who, having become pope, came to fear him. In fact, men offend either out of fear or out of hatred. Those he had offended were, among others, San Piero ad Vincula, Colonna, San Giorgio, and Ascanio; all the others, having become popes, had to fear him, except Rouen, by power and by having the kingdom of France at its side, and the Spanish, by affinity and obligations. Consequently, the duke, first of all, had to ensure that a Spanish pope was elected, and, failing that, he had to consent to the election of the cardinal of Rouen and not that of San Piero ad Vincula. And the one who believes that new benefits will cause great characters to forget old injuries is deceived. The duke made a mistake in this election, becoming himself the cause of his ruin.

CHAPTER VIII
CONCERNING THOSE WHO OBTAINED A PRINCIPALITY BY TREACHEROUS MEANS
(De his qui per scelera ad principatum pervenere)

One can become a prince in two ways that cannot be totally attributed to fortune or virtue; it does not seem right to put them apart, even though one of them can be considered more widely when we talk about republics.

These ways are either when, by any criminal and treacherous means, one ascends to the principality, or when a private citizen becomes prince of his fatherland with the favor of his fellow citizens. And, talking about the first way, I will point out two examples – one ancient, one modern – without, however, going into the merits of this part, as I think that anyone who needs it will just have to imitate them.

Agathocles, from Sicily, not only of private status but also of a low and abject condition, became king of Syracuse. This man, the son of a potter, always had a criminal life throughout his youth; however, he accompanied his criminal acts with such strength of mind and body that, having joined the militia, due to acts of evil, he became praetor of Syracuse. Being established in that position, and having decided to become a prince and maintain by violence and without the favor of others what had been granted to him by everyone's agreement, afterward, regarding his wish, he established an agreement with Hamilcar, the Carthaginian, who was in action with his armies in Sicily. One morning he gathered the people and the senate of Syracuse together as if he had to deliberate with them about matters relating to the republic, and, at a given signal, the soldiers killed all the senators and the richest people of the city. After these deaths, he occupied and maintained the principality of that city without any civil controversy. And, although the Carthaginians had broken with him twice and established siege, he was not only able to defend his city but, having left part of his people in the defense against the siege, with the others he attacked Africa and in a short time freed Syracuse of the siege, taking the Carthaginians to extreme difficulty: they had to establish an agreement with him and be content with the possessions of Africa, leaving Sicily to Agathocles.

Whoever considers, therefore, the actions and life of this prince, will not find anything, or little that can be attributed to fortune: his actions resulted, as said above, not from someone's favor but from his rise in the militia, obtained with a thousand troubles and dangers, which allowed him to achieve the principality and, later, maintain it with so many courageous and risky decisions. Yet it cannot be called virtue to kill fellow citizens, to betray friends, to be without faith, without mercy, without religion; such ways may gain power but not glory. Furthermore, if one considers the virtue of Agathocles in entering and exiting dangers and the greatness of his spirit in enduring and overcoming adversities, one will not find why he should be judged inferior to any of the most excellent captains; however, his exacerbated cruelty and inhumanity, with countless perversities, do not allow him to be celebrated among the most illustrious men. One cannot, therefore, attribute to fortune or virtue what he achieved; there is not one without the other.

In our times, during the rule of Alexander VI, Oliverotto of Fermo, having been fatherless years before, was raised by a maternal uncle called Giovanni Fogliani; in the early years of his youth, he was sent to military life under the command of Pagolo Vitelli, so that, having taken that discipline, he could reach an excellent position in the militia. After Pagolo died, he fought under his brother Vitellozzo, and in a very short time, being ingenious with a strong physique and mind, he became the first man in his militia. But, as it seemed to him a servile thing to be under the orders of others, with the help of some citizens of Fermo, to whom servitude was more precious than the freedom of their country, and with the favor of Vitellozzo, he thought of occupying Fermo. And he wrote to Giovanni Fogliani saying that, having been away from home for many years, he wanted to visit him, see his city again, and get to know its heritage. As he had only worked to gain honor, so that his fellow citizens could see how he had not spent his time in vain, he wanted to arrive with pomp and accompanied by a hundred horses, his friends and servants. He asked his uncle to be received by the citizens of Fermo with all the honors, so that it would not only dignify him but also Fogliani, as he had been his disciple.

Giovanni did not stop expending efforts in favor of his nephew; having made the residents of Fermo receive him with honors, he accommodated him in his own house. Then, after a few days and having arranged what was necessary for his wicked designs, Oliverotto promoted a very solemn feast to which he invited Giovanni Fogliani and all the chiefs of Fermo. Once the delicacies were consumed and all the other usual entertainment on similar occasions were finished, Oliverotto skillfully addressed certain serious subjects, speaking of the greatness of Pope Alexander, his son Cesare, and their undertakings. Having Giovanni and the others answered to such considerations, he suddenly stood up, saying that it was a matter to be discussed in a more secret place, retiring to a room where Giovanni and all the others went after him. They had not even sat down yet, when soldiers came out from hidden places and killed Giovanni and everyone else.

After this massacre, Oliverotto mounted his horse, ran through the city accompanied by his men, and besieged the supreme magistrate in his palace; consequently, out of fear, they were forced to obey him and form a government of which he made himself prince. And, having killed all those who, because they were discontent, could injure him, he strengthened himself with new civil and military orders so that, during the period of one year in which he retained the principality, he was not only strong in the city of Fermo but also became a cause of terror for all neighboring populations. And his destruction would have been as difficult as that of Agathocles if he had not been deceived by Cesare Borgia when he, in Senigallia, as it was already said, imprisoned the Orsini and the Vitelli. There he was also arrested and strangled together with Vitellozzo, master of his disloyalties, a year after committing the parricide.

Some may wonder how it can happen that Agathocles and others like him, after so many betrayals and cruelties, were able to live for a long time, without danger, in their fatherland and, even, defend themselves against external enemies without their fellow citizens having conspired against them, all the more seeing that many others were unable to maintain the state by means of cruelty in peaceful times, and, much less, in doubtful times of war. I think this is the result of cruelty being badly or improperly used. Properly used is applied to those (if it is possible to speak well of evil) that are done instantly due to the need to establish oneself, and afterward they are not insisted on but rather transformed into the maximum possible usefulness for the subjects. Badly used are those that, although few at first, increase over time instead of becoming extinct. Those who observe the first way of acting can remedy their situation with the support of God and men, as happened with Agathocles; it becomes impossible for those who follow the other way to continue in power.

Therefore, it should be noted that, when occupying a state, the conqueror must exercise all those injuries that become necessary, doing them all at the same time so as not to have to renew them every day, and to be able, thus, to give safety to men and win them to himself with benefits. The one who acts differently, either from shyness or bad advice, always needs to keep the knife in his hand and can never trust his subjects, as they cannot trust him in the face of new and continuous injuries. Therefore, injuries must be done all at once, so that, if tasted little, they offend less, while benefits must be done little by little, so that they can be better appreciated. Above all, a prince must live with his subjects in such a way that no unexpected circumstances, good or bad, make him change, because when the need arises in adverse times, he will not be in time to do evil, and the good that is done will not be useful to him since, if considered forced, it will not bring gratitude.

CHAPTER IX
Concerning a civil principality
(De principatu civili)

When a private citizen, not by betrayal or other intolerable violence, but by the favor of his fellow citizens, becomes prince of his country, what may be called a civil principality (to become so, not much virtue or fortune is necessary, but rather a fortunate cunning), I say that one ascends to this principality either by the favor of the people or by the favor of the nobles. Because these two diverse tendencies are found in every city, and this results from the fact that the people do not want to be commanded or oppressed by the powerful, and these want to rule and oppress the people. It is from these two diverse longings that one of the three effects arises in cities: principality, freedom, or anarchy.

A principality is constituted either by the people or by the nobles, depending on whether one or the other of these parts has the opportunity. The nobles, seeing they cannot withstand the people, begin to lend prestige to one of them and make him a prince so that they can, under his shadow, give expansion to their ambitions. The people, seeing that they cannot withstand the nobles, turn their esteem to a citizen and make him a prince so that they can be defended by his authority. The one who comes to the principality with the help of the nobles maintains himself with more difficulty than the one who comes to it with the support of the people because if he comes to the principality with many around him who seem to be his equals, he can neither rule nor manage them to his liking.

But the one who comes to the principality with popular support finds himself there alone, and there is no one around him or very few are not prepared to obey him. In addition, without injury to others, one cannot honestly satisfy the nobles, but one can satisfy the people, as their objective is more honest than that of the nobles, with the latter wanting to oppress while the former just wanting not to be oppressed.

A prince can never secure himself against the enmity of the people, as there are many of them. Against the nobles, however, he can secure himself because they are few. The worst thing a prince can expect from a hostile people is to be abandoned by them; but from hostile nobles, not only must he fear being abandoned, but he must also fear that they will turn against him, since, as they have more vision and greater cunning, they always have time to save themselves and seek to acquire prestige from the one they expect to prevail. Furthermore, the prince must necessarily always live with the same people, while he can live well without those same nobles, since he can make and unmake his power every day, giving or taking away their reputation, at his pleasure.

The nobles must be considered in two main groups: either they behave in such a way as to subject themselves entirely to the prince's fortune, or they act on their own. Those who subject to it and are not greedy should be honored and loved. Those who do not submit must be seen in two ways: if they do so out of cowardice or a natural defect of spirit, one should make use of them, mainly because they are good advisors, because in prosperity, this will honor the prince, and in adversity, he will not need to fear them. But when they cunningly do not submit themselves out of ambition, it is a sign that they think more about themselves than about the prince. From these, he must guard himself, fearing them as if they were declared enemies, because always, in adversity, they will help to ruin him.

Someone who becomes a prince through the favor of the people must preserve them as friends, which becomes easy, since they only ask not to be oppressed. But whoever becomes a prince through the favor of the nobles against the people must firstly seek to win them for himself, which becomes easy when he assumes their protection. And because men, when receiving good from whom they were expecting evil, subject themselves more to their benefactor, the people immediately become more devoted to him than if he had been raised to the principality by their favors. The prince can win the affection of the people in many ways, but as they vary according to the circumstances, one cannot establish a certain rule, which is why we will not consider them.

A prince needs to have the people as friends; otherwise, he will have no chance in adversity. Nabis, prince of the Spartans, endured the siege of all Greece and a Roman army full of victories, defending his fatherland and state against them. It was enough for him, when danger came, to protect himself against a few, which would not be enough if he had the people as his enemies. And let no one come along to refute my opinion with that well-known proverb: "He who builds on the people, builds on the mud." This is true only when a private citizen establishes foundations there and persuades himself that the people will free him when he is oppressed by his enemies or by the magistrates. In this case, it would be possible to feel frequently deceived, like the Gracchi in Rome and Monsignor Giorgio Scali in Florence. But if he is a prince who relies on the people, who can command, and is a man of courage, who does not weaken in adversity, does not lack weapons, and keeps the entire people encouraged with his courage and determination, he will never find himself deceived, and it will be shown that he laid his foundations well.

These principalities are often in danger when they are about to pass from civil order to absolute government because these princes either rule by themselves or through the magistrates. In the latter case, their situation is weaker and more dangerous, because they depend completely on the will of the citizens who are raised to magistracy and who, especially in adverse times, can destroy the government with great ease, either by intrigue or open defiance. And the prince cannot, in times of danger, assume absolute authority, because citizens and subjects, accustomed to receiving orders from magistrates, are not, in those circumstances, able to obey his determinations, and there will always be, in doubtful times, a lack of people he can trust.. Such a prince cannot base himself on what he observes in times of peace, when citizens need the state, because then everyone runs, everyone promises, and everyone wants to die for him while death is far away; but in adversity, at a time when the state needs citizens, then few are found. And this experiment is all the more dangerous because it can only be carried out once. However, a skillful prince must think of the way in which he can ensure that his citizens always, and in any circumstances, have need of the state and of himself, and they will always be faithful to him.

CHAPTER X
How should the strength of all principalities be measured?
(Quomodo omnium principatuum vires perpendi debeant)

When examining the modalities of these principalities, it is worth making one more consideration: whether the prince of a very powerful state would be able, if necessary, to support himself, or he would always need the protection of others. To better clarify this part, I believe that those who can, through an abundance of men and money, organize an army equal to the danger they face and face a battle against whoever comes to attack them, are able to support themselves, as well as those in need of the defense of others who cannot face the enemy in the open field and are forced to take refuge behind the city walls, garrisoning them. As for the first case, it has already been discussed, and in the future we will say what is necessary. Regarding the second case, nothing more can be proved than to urge these princes to fortify and provide for their city, not worrying about the territory that surrounds it.

Whoever has his city well-fortified and has managed the concerns of his subjects, as it was previously said and will later become clear, will never be attacked without great caution, because men are always enemies of undertakings where difficulties can be seen and ease cannot be found to attack anyone who has a fortified city and is not hated by his people.

The cities of Germany enjoy great freedom, have little territory, and obey the emperor when they want. They do not fear either this or any other power around them because they are so fortified that everyone thinks it must be boring and difficult to submit and dominate them. In fact, they all have proper moats and walls, they have sufficient artillery, and they always keep in public depots what is necessary to drink, eat, and stay warm for a year. Furthermore, to keep the people fed without harming the state, they always have, in common, for a year, means to give them work in those activities that are the life and strength of the cities and industries from which people feed. They have a high regard for military exercises, regarding which they have many regulatory laws.

A prince, therefore, who has a strong city and does not make himself hated, cannot be attacked, and if there were someone who attacked him, it would retreat in shame. Again, the things of this world are so changeable that it is almost impossible to keep an army a whole year in the field without being interfered with. To anyone who replied that, having their properties outside the city and seeing them burn, the people will not have patience, and the long siege and self-pity will make them forget the prince, I would answer that a powerful and bold prince will always overcome those difficulties, sometimes giving his subjects hope that the evil will not last long, sometimes instilling fear of the enemy's cruelty, and sometimes deftly assuring himself of those who seem too reckless.

The enemy will try to ruin the country immediately after his arrival when the spirit of men is still fiery and willful in defense; therefore, the prince does not need to fear because, after a few days, when tempers are cooler, the damage is already done, the ills are incurred, and there is no longer any remedy; then, the subjects come to unite even more to their prince, seeming to them that he owes them an obligation since their houses were set on fire and their properties were ruined for his defense.

And the nature of men is that of obliging themselves as much by the benefits that are given as by those that are received. Hence, if everything is well considered, it will not be difficult for a wise prince to keep the spirits of his citizens steadfast, before and after the siege, as long as they do not lack food or means of defense.

CHAPTER XI
CONCERNING ECCLESIASTICAL PRINCIPALITIES
(De principatibus eclesiasticis)

Let's talk now about ecclesiastical principalities, covering all the difficulties found before conquering them, since they are acquired either by virtue or by fortune, and without one or the other they are preserved, because they are supported by ancient orders established in religion. These become so strong and of such a nature that they keep their princes always in power, no matter how they behave and live. Only these have states and do not defend them; they have subjects and do not rule them; and their states, although unguarded, are not taken from them. The subjects, because they are not ruled, do not worry, do not think, and cannot separate themselves from them. Only these principalities are safe and happy. But, since they are directed by a superior reason, which the human mind cannot reach, I will stop talking about them because, being exalted and maintained by God, it would be the work of a presumptuous and reckless man to talk about them. However, if anyone asks me where it comes from that the Church, in temporal power, has reached such greatness, since before Alexander the Italian potentates, and not only those who were called "potentates," but any baron and lord, even if without importance, little value they gave to the temporal power of the Church, and now a king of France trembles before it, and it can expel him from Italy and still manage to ruin the Venetians, I will point out facts that, despite being known, it does not seem superfluous to revive in part in memory.

Before Charles, King of France, invaded Italy, this province was under the rule of the Pope, the Venetians, the King of Naples, the Duke of Milan, and the Florentines. These potentates had to take two main precautions: one, that no foreigner should enter Italy with troops; and the other, that none of them should expand their domains.

Those who were most afraid were the pope and the Venetians. To restrain the Venetians, it became necessary the union of all the others, as occurred in the defense of Ferrara; to stop the pope, they used the barons of Rome, as they were divided into two factions, Orsini and Colonna, and there was always a reason for discord between them. And, with weapons in hand under the eyes of the pontiff, they kept the pontificate weak and insecure. If, from time to time, a spirited pope appeared, like Sixtus, neither his fortune nor his knowledge could free him from these inconveniences.

The short life of the pontiffs was the cause of this situation because, in the ten years that, on average, a pope lived, it was only with great difficulty that he could weaken one of the factions. If, for example, one of them had almost extinguished the Colonna, another one appeared, an enemy of the Orsini, who made them resurface without having time to ruin the Orsini. This made the temporal power of the pope little regarded in Italy.

Then came Alexander VI, who, of all the pontiffs that ever existed, was the one who showed how a pope could, with money and troops, acquire greater power. And he did, with the use of Duke Valentino as an instrument and with the opportunity of the invasion of the French, all those things that I reported previously regarding the actions of the duke.

Although his intention was not to make the Church great, but rather the Duke, nevertheless, everything he did contributed to the greatness of the Church, which, after his death and the ruin of the Duke, became the heir of all his work. Pope Julius came afterward and found the Church strong, possessing the entire Romagna, the barons of Rome reduced to impotence, and, through Alexander's persecutions, those factions have been wiped out. He also found the way open to accumulate money, which had never been done before Alexander.

Pope Julius II not only followed these practices, he expanded them; he thought of conquering Bologna, extinguishing the Venetians and expelling the French from Italy. All these undertakings turned out well for him, and so much more to his credit, as he did all this to strengthen the Church and not to favor any private citizen. He also kept the Orsini and Colonna parties in the same conditions in which he found them, and although there was a leader among them capable of changing the situation, two things kept them quiet: the greatness of the Church, which frightened them, and the fact that they do not have cardinals, which are the causes of the turmoil between the factions. Whenever these factions have their cardinals, they do not remain quiet for long, as they support the factions inside and outside Rome, and the barons are forced to defend them; thus, from the ambition of the prelates, discord and turmoil arise among the barons. His Holiness, Pope Leo, found the pontificate extremely powerful, and it is hoped that those to whom we refer made it great through weapons, and he will make it even greater and more venerated by his goodness and his other infinite virtues.

CHAPTER XII
HOW MANY KINDS OF MILITIAS ARE THERE? AND CONCERNING MERCENARIES

(Quot sint genera militiae et de mercenariis militibus)

I will now talk, in a generic way, about the offensive and defensive means that may occur in each of the aforementioned principalities. Previously, I talked in detail about all types of principalities, which I proposed to comment on at the beginning, and considered, in some points, the causes of their well-being and discomfort, showing that they were the ways in which many sought to acquire and preserve them.

We talk about how necessary it is for a prince to have good foundations; otherwise, he will necessarily fall into ruin. The main foundations that states have, whether new, old, or mixed, are good laws and good weapons. And, as there cannot be good laws where there are no good weapons, and where there are good weapons, there must be good laws. I will stop talking about laws and I will only refer to weapons.

The weapons with which a prince defends his state are either his own or mercenary, auxiliary, or mixed. Mercenaries and auxiliaries are useless and dangerous, and if someone has their state supported by mercenary troops, it will never be firm and safe because they are disunited, ambitious, undisciplined, unfaithful, valiant among friends, vile among enemies; they have no fear of God and no faith in men, and destruction is deferred only so long as the attack is; in peace one is plundered by them, in war by the enemies. The fact is, they have no other love or reason that keeps them in the field other than a little pay, which is not enough to make them want to die for you. They really want to be your soldiers while you are not at war, but when war comes, they take themselves off or run from the foe.

To convince someone of such things, I do not need to try very hard, since the current ruin of Italy was caused by no other factor than that of having, for many years, rested on mercenary weapons. They had already done something in favor of some and seemed valiant in fights among themselves, but when the foreigners came, they showed what they were. That is why it was possible for Charles, king of France, to take Italy easily, and the one who told us that our sins were the cause of it told the truth, although these sins were not those that he judged but rather those that I narrated, and as the princes were guilty, they suffered the punishment.

I want to better demonstrate the unfortunate quality of these troops. The mercenary captains are either excellent men or not: if they are, you cannot trust them because they will always aspire to their own greatness, slaughtering you, who are their master, or oppressing others against your will. But if they are not great captains, they will certainly lead you to ruin. And if it is answered that anyone who holds the forces in their hands will act in the same way, mercenary or not, I will reply by saying how weapons should be used by a prince or a republic. The prince must go in person with the troops and perform the captain's duties: the republic must send its citizens, and when it sends one who does not prove to be brave, it must replace him; when one becomes angry, it must stop him with the laws so that he does not advance beyond the limit. And experience has shown princes and republics, single-handedly, making the greatest progress, and mercenaries doing nothing except damage. And it is more difficult to bring a republic, armed with its own weapons, under the sway of one of its citizens than the republic that is protected by mercenary or auxiliary troops.

Rome and Sparta were, for many centuries, armed and free. The Swiss are very armed and extremely free. Of ancient mercenaries, we can mention as an example the Carthaginians, who were almost oppressed by their mercenary soldiers at the end of the first war with the Romans, despite having Carthage's own citizens as their leaders. Philip of Macedonia was made captain of his people by the Thebans after the death of Epaminondas, and after the victory, he took away their freedom. The Milanese, after the death of Duke Filippo, hired Francisco Sforza to fight the Venetians, and he, having defeated his enemies in Caravaggio, joined them to oppress the Milanese, his masters. Sforza, his father, being in the service of Queen Joanna of Naples, suddenly left her unarmed; therefore, in order not to lose her kingdom, she was forced to throw herself into the arms of the King of Aragon.

And if the Venetians and Florentines formerly extended their domains by these troops, and yet their captains did not make themselves princes, but have defended them, I clarify that the Florentines, in this case, were favored by chance, because of the able captains, whom they could fear, some did not win or had to fight against antagonists, others turned their ambition to different places. The one who did not win was Giovanni Acuto. Therefore, even though his loyalty cannot be known, everyone will agree that, if he had won, the Florentines would have been at his mercy. Sforza always had the Braccio against him, watching each other. Francesco turned his ambition to Lombardy and Braccio went against the Church and the kingdom of Naples. But let's look at what happened a short while ago. The Florentines made Pagolo Vitelli their captain, a man of great prudence who, in private life, had achieved a great reputation. If he conquered Pisa, there would be no one who could deny that it would be convenient for the Florentines to be under his orders, even because, if he had remained as a soldier of their enemies, they would have no means of resisting and, having him at their side, they would have to obey him.

The Venetians, if their progress is considered, will be seen to have acted safely and gloriously while they waged war alone (which was before they turned their sights to the land), and, with the support of the gentlemen and the armed plebeians, they acted with great courage. But as they started fighting on land, they abandoned this prudence and followed the war customs of Italy. At the beginning of their terrestrial expansion, as they did not have a very large state and because they enjoyed a high reputation, they did not need to fear their captains much. However, when they expanded their conquests, which occurred under Carmignola, they had proof of this mistake.

Therefore, having seen his value when under his command they defeated the Duke of Milan and, on the other hand, knowing how lukewarm he was in the war, they judged they would no longer conquer under him, given his bad will. Without being able to let him go, so as not to lose what they had acquired, they were compelled, in order to secure themselves, to kill him. They had, afterward, their captains Bartolomeo of Bergamo, Roberto of San Severino, the count of Pitigliano, and others like them, under whom they had to fear defeats and not their conquests, as happened later in Vaila, where, in a battle, they lost everything that, in eight hundred years, with so much work, had been conquered. In fact, these troops only result in slow, late, and weak conquests, but quick and miraculous losses. And, as I presented these examples of Italy, which has been, for many years, dominated by mercenary weapons, I want to analyze these troops in a more general way, so that, seeing their origin and development, one can better correct the mistake of their employment.

You must know that in recent years, the empire started being repelled in Italy, the pope started having a reputation for temporal power, and Italy was divided into several states. In fact, many of the largest cities took up weapons against their nobles, who, previously favored by the emperor, kept them oppressed, and the Church, to obtain a reputation in temporal power, favored them; in many others, their citizens became princes.

It turns out that, with almost all of Italy falling into the hands of the Church and some republics, and the Church consisting of priests and the republic of citizens not accustomed to the use of weapons, they started recruiting foreign mercenaries. The first person who gave fame to this militia was Alberigo da Conio, a native of Romagna, and from his weapons school came, among others, Braccio and Sforza, in their days the arbiters of Italy. After these came all the others who, until our time, led these troops, and the end of their value was that Italy found itself traversed by Charles, plundered by Louis, raped by Ferdinand, and dishonored by the Swiss.

The order they initially observed was – to give themselves a reputation – to take the concept away from the infantry. They did this because, as they were stateless and lived off the weapons industry, few infantrymen would not give them fame, and if there were many, they would not be able to feed them. In this way, they limited themselves to cavalry where, with bearable numbers, the troops could be nourished and honored. And, after all, the situation became such that, in an army of twenty thousand soldiers, there were not two thousand infantrymen. They had, besides this, used every means to keep fatigue and fear away from themselves and their soldiers, not killing in the battle but taking prisoners and liberating them without ransom. They did not attack the walled cities, and those in the cities did not attack the camps; they did not surround the camp either with a stockade or ditch, and they did not campaign in the winter. All these things were permitted by their military rules and devised by them, as it was said, to avoid fatigue and fear; thus, they dragged Italy into slavery and dishonor.

CHAPTER XIII
CONCERNING AUXILIARIES, MIXED AND OWN SOLDIERS
(De militibus auxiliariis, mixtis et propriis)

Auxiliary troops, which are the other useless forces, are employed when a powerful person is called with their forces to help and defend, as Pope Julius II did in recent times. Having seen in the Ferrara campaign the sad figure of his mercenary troops, turned to his auxiliaries and reached an agreement with Ferdinand, king of Spain, for his assistance with men and weapons. These auxiliary troops can be useful and good for themselves, but for those who call them, they are almost always harmful; for losing, one is undone, and for winning, one is their captive.

Even though ancient histories are full of these examples, I do not want to abandon this recent lesson from Pope Julius II, whose decision to hand himself entirely into the hands of a foreigner, because he wanted to conquer Ferrara, could not have been more foolish. But his good fortune caused a third event to arise so that he did not reap the results of his bad choice; his auxiliaries being defeated in Ravenna and the Swiss appearing and, against the expectations of Pope Julius II and others, expelled the conquerors, the pope did not become a prisoner either of the conquerors, who fled, nor of his auxiliary troops, for having won with weapons other than their own.

The Florentines, being completely unarmed, took ten thousand Frenchmen to Pisa to attack it, by which decision they were in greater danger than at any time during their own work. The emperor of Constantinople, to oppose his neighbors, concentrated ten thousand Turks in Greece who, after the war, did not want to leave the country, which constituted the beginning of Greece's subjection to the infidels.

Therefore, whoever does not want to win, make use of these troops that are much more dangerous than the mercenaries, as with these troops ruin is certain, given that they are all united, all dedicated to obedience to others. The mercenaries, in order to harm you after victory, contrary to what happens with the mixed ones, need more time and greater opportunity, not only because they do not constitute a whole, but also because they were organized and paid by you; yet, with their leader constituting a third party, he does not obtain enough authority for this. In conclusion, while in mercenary troops the most dangerous thing is cowardice, in auxiliaries it is valor.

A wise prince, therefore, has always avoided these troops, turning to his own forces, preferring to lose with his own rather than win with the others, since, in truth, victory would not represent a real one if conquered with other people's weapons. I will never hesitate to mention Cesare Borgia and his actions as an example. This duke entered Romagna with auxiliary troops, leading only the French forces there, and with them taking

Imola and Forli. But then, as these weapons no longer seemed reliable, he turned to the mercenaries, believing he found less danger in them; and took into his service the Orsini and Vitelli. Later, after handling these forces and finding them doubtful, unfaithful, and dangerous, he extinguished them and turned to his own troops. And the difference between one and the other of these forces can easily be seen when one considers the difference there was in the reputation of the duke, when he had only the French and then the Orsini and Vitelli, and when he trusted his own soldiers; his prestige increased, and he was only loved enough when everyone saw that he was the absolute master of his troops.

Without abandoning the Italian and more recent examples, I do not want to forget Hiero of Syracuse, one of those previously mentioned by me. This man, as I said, made head of the armies by the Syracusans, soon recognized that mercenary troops were not useful, as their leaders were identical to Italian ones; as it seemed to him that he could neither keep them nor let them go, he had them all cut into pieces, and then started waging war with his own troops and not with those of others. I also want to bring to mind an instance from the Old Testament applicable to this subject. David offered himself to Saul to fight with Goliath, the Philistine champion, and, to give him courage, Saul armed him with his own weapons, which, once put on by David, were rejected by him: with them, he could not rely well on himself, preferring to face the enemy with just his sling and his knife. In conclusion, the weapons of others either fall from your back or they weigh you down and embarrass you.

Charles VII, father of Louis XI, having freed France from the English by his fortune and virtue, knew this need to arm himself with his own forces, and organized cavalry and infantry weapons in his kingdom on a regular basis. Later, King Louis, his son, extinguished the infantry and started enticing the Swiss, a mistake that, followed by others, became, as we now see, the reason for the dangers of that kingdom.

In fact, by giving the Swiss a reputation, Louis diminished the value of all his troops, since he extinguished the infantry forces and subordinated his cavalry to someone else's militia, and the latter, accustomed to fighting with the Swiss, seemed unable to win without them. Hence, it arises that the French cannot stand against the Swiss and, without the Swiss, they do not try to fight against the others. The armies of France, therefore, have been mixed, partly mercenaries and partly their own troops, forces that, together, are much better than simple auxiliaries or merely mercenaries, but much inferior to one's own forces. The example mentioned is enough, as the kingdom of France would be invincible if Charles's military organization had been developed or preserved. But men's lack of wisdom often begins with something that seems good, without realizing the poison it hides, as I have already said about tuberculosis.

Therefore, if the one who rules a principality does not know evils until they are upon him, he is not truly wise; and this insight is given to few. And, if one considers the beginning of the ruin of the Roman Empire, it will be seen that it resulted from the simple beginning of the enticement of the Goths, since it was then that the forces of the Roman Empire started declining and all that value which had raised it passed away to others. I conclude, therefore, that without having its own weapons, no principality is safe. On the contrary, it is completely subject to fortune, with no virtue that can defend it in adversity. And it has always been the opinion and sentence of wise men that *quod nihil sit tam infirmum aut instabile, quam fama potentiae non sua vi nixa* (nothing is so unstable as the fame or power of a prince when it is not supported by his own strength).

And one's own forces are those that are made up either of subjects, citizens, or dependents; all others are mercenaries or auxiliaries. The way to organize one's own troops will be easy to find if one analyzes the organization of the four mentioned by me, and if one considers how Philip, father

> "Men's lack of wisdom often begins with something that seems good, without realizing the poison it hides."

of Alexander the Great, and many republics and principalities, armed and organized themselves. I entirely commit myself to these organizations.

CHAPTER XIV
WHAT CONCERNS A PRINCE ABOUT THE MILITIA?
(Quod principem deceat circa militiam)

A prince must have no other objective or thought, nor take anything else to do other than war and its organization and discipline, since that is the only art that belongs to the one who rules. And it is of such virtue that it not only keeps those who were born princes, but it also often makes them rise from a private status to that position; on the contrary, it is seen that, when princes think more about delicacies than weapons, they lose their states. The first reason that makes you lose the government is neglecting this art, while the reason that allows you to conquer it is to be a master in this art.

It was because he was armed that the private citizen Francisco Sforza became Duke of Milan, and the sons, through avoiding the hardships and troubles of weapons, from dukes became private citizens. In fact, among other evils that being unarmed brings you, it makes you despicable, which constitutes one of those infamies that the prince must guard against, as will be explained below.

In fact, there is no proportion between an armed prince and an unarmed one, and it is not reasonable for the armed one to willingly obey the unarmed one, nor for the unarmed one to feel safe among armed servants. Because, if there is disdain on the part of one and suspicion on the other's side, it is not possible for them to act well together. Furthermore, a prince who does not understand the art of war, in addition to the other misfortunes already mentioned, suffers from not being able to be liked by his soldiers and not being able to trust them.

Therefore, the prince must not divert his thoughts for a moment from the exercise of war, which he can do in two ways: one with action and the other with the mind. As for action, in addition to keeping his troops well organized and exercised, he must always be on hunts to accustom his body to fatigue and, in part, to get to know the nature of the places and know how mountains arise, how valleys open out, how the plains stretch out, and learn the nature of the rivers and marshes, paying close attention to it all.

This knowledge is useful for two reasons: first, he learns to know his own country and can better identify the defenses it offers; then, as a result of the knowledge and observation of those places, he understands with ease any other which it may be necessary for him to study hereafter, such as the hills, valleys, plains, rivers, and marshes that exist. For example, in Tuscany, there is a certain similarity with those of other provinces so that, with a knowledge of the aspects of one province, one can easily move on to those of other provinces. The prince who is deficient in this skill is devoid of the main element that a captain needs, as it teaches him how to find the enemy, establish camps, lead armies, order journeys, and make incursions across lands with an advantage over the enemy.

Philopoemen, prince of the Achaeans, among the praise given to him by writers, also deserved the one that, in times of peace, he never had anything in his mind but the rules of war, and, when touring the fields with his friends, he often stopped and argued with them:

"If the enemies were on that hill and we were here with our army, which of us would have the advantage? How could we attack them while maintaining troop formation? If we wanted to withdraw, how should we proceed? If they withdrew, how would we pursue them?" And he presented to them, as he walked, all the cases that could occur in an army;

> *"Therefore, the prince must not divert his thoughts for a moment from the exercise of war."*

he listened to their opinions, and gave his own, corroborating them with arguments in such a way that, due to these continuous considerations, he could never, commanding the armies, find any unforeseen event for which he had no solution.

However, as for the exercise of the mind, the prince must read the stories and observe in them the actions of great men, see how they conducted themselves in wars, and examine the causes of their victories and defeats, so as to be able to escape those responsible for these and imitate the causes of those; he must do, above all, as in times gone by, some great men did, imitating everyone who was praised and glorified before them, and always had within themselves their achievements and deeds, as it is said that Alexander the Great imitated Achilles, Caesar to Alexander, and Scipio to Cyrus. Whoever reads the life of Cyrus, written by Xenophon, realizes later, in the life of Scipio, how much that imitation brought him glory, as well as how much in chastity, affability, humanity, and liberality Scipio resembled what Xenophon wrote about Cyrus.

A wise prince must observe this similarity of procedure, never being idle in times of peace, but rather, with skill, trying to build up resources to be able to use them in adversity, so that, when fortune changes, he will be prepared to resist.

CHAPTER XV
CONCERNING THINGS FOR WHICH MEN, AND ESPECIALLY PRINCES, ARE PRAISED FOR OR BLAMED
(De his rebus quibus homines, et praesertim principes, laudantur aut vituperantur)

It remains now to see what the manners and behavior of a prince should be towards his subjects and friends and because I know that many have already written about it, I expect I shall be considered presumptuous by writing on the same subject, especially when I will compete this matter with the guidance already given by others to the princes. But, as my intention is to write something useful for those who are interested in this, it seemed more convenient to go in search of the truth extracted from the facts and not from the ramblings about them, as many have conceived of republics and principalities never seen or known.

There is so much difference between how one lives and how one should live that the one who abandons what is done for what should be done will learn the path of his ruin rather than the path of his preservation, for a man who wants in all his words to make a profession of kindness will be lost among so many who are not good. Hence, it is necessary for a prince who wants to maintain himself to learn how to not be good and whether or not to use kindness, according to need.

Putting aside, therefore, matters relating to an imaginary prince and talking about those that are true, I say that all men, especially princes situated in a more prominent position, when analyzed, stand out for some of those attributes that bring them either blame or praise. Thus, it is that some are said to be liberal, some miserable (using a Tuscan term, because an "avaricious" person in our language is still the one who desires to possess by robbery, while "miserly" we call the one who abstains excessively from using what he possesses); some are considered prodigals, some thieves; some cruel, some merciful; one disloyal, another faithful; one fragile and cowardly, another fierce and brave; one human, another superb; one lascivious, another chaste; one simple, another cunning; one hard, another easy; one serious, another frivolous; one religious, another unbeliever, and so on.

I know that each one will confess that it would be extremely praiseworthy to find in a prince, of all the attributes mentioned above, only those that are considered good; but, since they cannot possess them nor fully observe them because human contingencies do not allow it, it is necessary for the prince to be so prudent that he knows how to escape the infamy of those vices that would make him lose power, taking care to avoid even those that would not put his position at risk; but, not being able to avoid it, it is possible to tolerate them, although with a breach of due respect. Furthermore, do not prevent the prince from incurring the evil fate of those vices that, without them, it will be difficult to save the state; for, if everything is well considered, there will always be something that appears to be a virtue, but if practiced, will bring ruin, and something else that appears to be a vice, but if followed, will give rise to security and well-being.

CHAPTER XVI
Concerning Liberality and Parsimony
(De liberalitate et parsimonia)

Starting, then, with the first qualities I mentioned, I say that it would be good for the prince to be considered liberal; however, liberality used in such a way that it becomes known to everyone harms you, so if it is used virtuously and as it should be used, it will not be known and therefore the reputation of the opposite will not be avoided; however, wanting to maintain the name of liberal among men, it is necessary not to forget any type of sumptuousness, in such a way that a prince acting in this way will consume all his finances in ostentation and will need, in the end, if he wants to maintain the liberal concept, burden people extraordinarily with taxes and do everything he can use to get money. This will soon make him hateful to his subjects and, impoverishing him, will make him little esteemed by everyone; so that, having offended many and rewarded few with his liberality, he feels more intensely any initial setback and finds himself facing the first danger. Realizing this and wanting to retreat, the prince immediately incurs the bad reputation of being miserable.

A prince, not being able to use this liberal quality without suffering harm, making it known, must be wise. He must not worry about being seen as miserable, because, as time goes by, he will be considered more liberal. Since the people see that with his parsimony, the revenue is enough for them, and he can defend himself against anyone who would wage war against him and is able to carry out projects without burdening his people; in doing so, he comes to use liberality towards all those from whom he takes nothing, who are numerous, and to employ meanness towards all others to whom he does not give, who are few. In our times we have not seen great achievements except by those who were called miserable, while we have seen others become extinct.

Pope Julius used his reputation as a liberal to reach the papacy, but he did not think about keeping it so he could wage war. The present king of France waged so many wars without imposing an extraordinary tribute on his subjects, only because he superimposed his parsimony on superfluous expenses. The present king of Spain, if he was considered liberal, would not have accomplished or won so many undertakings.

Therefore, a prince must spend little so as not to rob his subjects, to be able to defend himself, so as not to become poor and despised, in order not to be forced to become a swindler, not minding incurring the reputation of being miserable, because this is one of those defects that make him reign. And if someone said that Caesar achieved the Empire by liberality, not to mention many others that have been or are considered liberal and have reached very high positions, I would answer: either you are already a prince or you are about to become one. In the first case this liberality is harmful; in the second one, it is quite necessary to be considered liberal. Caesar was one of those who wanted to ascend to the principality of Rome, but if, after reaching it, he had lived and had not used restraint in his expenses, he would have destroyed the Empire. And if someone replied that there were many princes, considered extremely liberal, who accomplished great things with their armies, I would answer: either the prince spends from his own, or from his subjects, or from someone else; in the first case, he must be parsimonious; in others, he must not fail to practice any liberality.

And that prince who goes with the armies, who supports himself by pillaging, looting, and ransoming, handling other people's goods, needs this liberality because, otherwise, he will not be followed by his soldiers. And of what is not yours or of your subjects, you can be the most generous giver, as were Cyrus, Caesar, and Alexander, because spending what belongs to others does not take away your reputation; on the contrary, it increases it. It is only spending your own that injures you. And there is nothing that destroys itself as much as liberality, because while you use it, you lose the ability to use it, becoming poor and despised, or, to escape poverty, a thief and hateful. And a prince should guard himself, above all things, against being despised and hated, and liberality leads you to both. Therefore, it is wiser to have the reputation of being miserable, which gives rise to infamy without hatred, than, because someone wants the concept of liberal, to find himself having to incur the judgment of a swindler, who creates a bad reputation with hatred.

CHAPTER XVII
Cruelty and mercy, and whether it is better to be loved than feared, or rather feared than loved

(De crudelitate et pietate; et an sit melius amari quam timeri, vel e contra)

Returning to other qualities already mentioned, I say that each prince must wish to be seen as merciful and not as cruel; despite this, he must be careful not to misuse this mercy. Cesare Borgia was considered cruel; however, his cruelty had recovered Romagna, managing to unite it and put it in peace and loyalty. Which, if considered correctly, will show that he was much more merciful than the Florentine people who, to escape the reputation of being cruel, allowed Pistoia to be destroyed. A prince should not, therefore, fear the bad reputation of being cruel, as long as he keeps his subjects united and loyal, since, with few examples, he will be more merciful than those who, due to excessive mercy, allow turmoil to arise, which results in murders or robberies, because these tend to harm the entire community, while those executions that originate with a prince affect only one individual. And, among all the princes, it is impossible for the new prince to avoid the label of cruel, since the new states are full of dangers. Virgil says, the mouth of Dido: *Res dura, et regni novitas me talia cogunt moliri, et late fines custo de tueri* (Against my will, my fate /

A throne unsettled, and an infant state / Bid me defend my realms with all my powers, / And guard with these severities my shores).

The prince, however, must be slow in believing and acting, not be alarmed by himself, and proceed in a balanced way, with prudence and humanity, seeking to prevent excessive confidence from making him incautious and too much distrust from making him intolerable.

A question then arises: whether it is better to be loved than feared or feared than loved? The answer is that it would be necessary to be one thing and another; but, as it is difficult to bring them together if one of the two is missing, it is much safer to be feared than loved. This is because, of men, it can generally be said that they are ungrateful, fickle, false, fearful of danger, and ambitious of gain; and, as long as you do them well, they are all yours, they offer you their blood, their goods, their lives, their children, as long as, as said above, the need is far distant; but when it approaches, however, they turn against you.

And the prince who trusted entirely in their words, finding himself devoid of other means of defense, is lost: friendships that are acquired by money and not by greatness and nobility of soul, are bought, but with them, it is not possible to count, and, at the right time, it is not possible to use them. And men have less scruple in offending someone who is beloved than someone who is feared, since friendship is maintained by a bond of obligation that, because men are bad, is broken at every opportunity that suits them, but fear is maintained by a dread of punishment that is never abandoned.

The prince must, however, make himself feared so that, if he does not conquer love, he escapes from hatred, especially because being feared and not being hated can very well coexist. This will always ensure that he refrains from taking the property and women of his citizens and subjects, and if it is necessary to shed someone's blood, he must do it when there is a proper justification and clear cause. Above all, he must keep his hands off the property of others, because men more quickly forget the death of their father than the loss of their patrimony.

Furthermore, there is never a lack of reasons to justify expropriations, and anyone who begins to live by robbery always finds reasons to take possession of other people's property, while the reasons for shedding blood are more difficult to find and sooner lapse.

But when the prince is at the head of his armies and has a multitude of soldiers under his command, then it is absolutely necessary not to care about the reputation of cruelty, because, without it, an army will never be kept united nor ready to fight. Among the wonderful deeds of Hannibal, this is worth mentioning: having a huge army, made up of men of countless races, led to battle in foreign lands; no dissension ever arose between them or against the prince, both in bad and in good fortune. This cannot result from anything other than that inhuman cruelty, which, combined with his countless virtues, always made him venerated and terrible in the opinion of his soldiers; without that cruelty, his virtues would not have been enough to produce such an effect, and, however, writers who are not very thoughtful about this, admire, on the one hand, his actions and, on the other, condemn the main cause of them.

To prove that, indeed, his other virtues were not enough, we can consider the case of Scipio, a most notable man, not only in his times but also in the memory of all known facts, whose armies rebelled in Spain as a result of his excessive mercy, as he had granted his soldiers more liberties than was appropriate to military discipline. This fact was reproved in the Senate by Fabius Maximus, who called him a corrupter of the Roman militia. The Locrians, having been ruined and slaughtered by a legate

"The prince must, however, make himself feared so that, if he does not conquer love, he escapes from hatred, especially because being feared and not being hated can very well coexist"

of Scipio, were not avenged by him, nor was the insolence of that legate repressed, all this resulting from his easy nature; insomuch that, wanting someone to excuse him before the Senate, he said there were many men who knew better not to make mistakes than to correct them. This disposition, if he had been continued in command, would have destroyed in time the fame and glory of Scipio; but, living under the government of the Senate, this harmful quality not only disappeared but contributed to his glory.

Returning to the question of being feared or loved, I come to the conclusion that, men loving according to their own will and fearing according to that of the prince, a wise prince should establish himself on what is under his own control and not under that of others; he must endeavor only to avoid hatred, as it was said.

CHAPTER XVIII
IN WHAT WAY SHOULD PRINCES KEEP FAITH IN THE WORD GIVEN?
(Quomodo fides a principibus sit servanda)

Everyone knows how praiseworthy it is when a prince keeps faith (in the given word) and lives with integrity, and not with cunning. However, experience shows that it is the princes who accomplished great deeds, giving little importance to the given word, and involved the minds of men with cunning, who surpassed those who were based on their word.

You must know, then, that there are two ways of fighting: one by the law, the other by force. The first way is proper for man; the second, for animals. But, as the first way is often not enough, it is necessary to resort to the second. Therefore, it is necessary for a prince to know how to avail himself of the animal and the man. This subject, in fact, was taught to the princes, covertly, by ancient writers, who describe how Achilles and many princes of old were left in the care of the centaur Chiron, which means solely that, having as master a being half animal and half man, that it is necessary for a prince to know how to make use of both natures: if the first is not enough, it is worth resorting to the second.

As it is necessary for a prince to know how to use animal nature, he must take the fox and the lion as models, because the lion cannot defend itself from snares and the fox has no defense against wolves. Therefore, it is necessary to be a fox to discover the snares and a lion to terrify the wolves. Those who act only like the lion do not know what they are about. Therefore, a wise lord cannot and should not keep his word when it is harmful to his interests and when the reasons that caused him to pledge it no longer exist.

If all men were good, this precept would be bad. But because they are bad and do not keep their word to the prince, there is no reason for him to keep it to them. A prince never lacked legitimate reasons to justify breaking his word. One could give countless modern examples of this, showing how many treaties and how many promises were frustrated and in vain due to the infidelity of princes, and the one who, most perfectly, knew how to act like the fox, did better. But it is necessary to know well how to disguise this quality and be a great pretender and dissembler. Men are so simple and so subject to present needs that whoever deceives will always find those who allow themselves to be deceived.

I do not want to fail to point out one of the recent examples. Alexander VI did nothing else but deceive men, and that was all he thought about. He always found occasion to deceive. There was never a man who had greater confidence in asserting, and who, with greater oaths, affirmed something that he later did not fulfill. However, mistakes always happened to him of his own free will, because he knew this aspect of the world well.

For a prince, therefore, it is not essential to possess all the qualities mentioned, but it is necessary to appear to possess them. Or better yet, I will dare to say that, possessing and always using them, they are harmful, while, appearing to possess them, they are useful. For example: appearing merciful, faithful, human, upright, religious, and actually being so. But be prepared and willing in spirit so that, if you need not to be, you can and know how to become the opposite. It must be understood that a prince, and in particular a new prince, cannot practice all those things for which men are considered good, since he is often forced to maintain the state, to act against the faith, against charity, against humanity, and against religion. However, he must have a spirit willing to turn according to the winds of fortune and the variations of facts that force him and, as it was said, not to depart from the good if he can, but to know how to enter into the bad if necessary.

A prince, therefore, must be very careful not to let anything slip from his mouth that is not full of the five qualities mentioned above, that he may appear to the one who sees and hears him altogether as merciful, faithful, human, upright, and religious. And there is nothing more necessary to be related than this last quality. It is just that men in general judge more by their eyes than by their hands, because it is up to everyone to see, but few are capable of feeling. Everyone sees what you appear to be; few feel what you are; and these few do not dare to contradict the opinion of the many who, in fact, are protected by the majesty of the state. In the actions of all men, and especially of princes, where there is no court to appeal to, what matters is their success. So let the prince do his best to win and maintain the state. The means will always be judged honorable and praised by everyone, because the people are always taken by appearances and results, and in the world, there is nothing but the people. The few cannot exist when the many have something to lean on. Some princes of present times, which it are not necessary to name, preach nothing but peace and faith, but of both he is a bitter enemy, and either, if he had kept it, would have deprived him of reputation and kingdom more than once.

CHAPTER XIX
How to avoid being despised and hated
(De contemptu et odio fugiendo)

As I already talked about the most important qualities mentioned, I wish to briefly discuss the others, under these generalities: that the prince must consider, as has been in part said before, how to avoid those circumstances that could make him hateful and despicable; whenever he does so, he will have fulfilled his part and will not find any danger in other defects.

Above all, as I have said, he will be hated if he is greedy and usurps the property and women of his subjects, from both of which he must abstain. And when neither their property nor their honor is touched, they will live happily, and it will only be necessary to fight the ambition of a few, which is restrained in many ways and with ease.

What makes him despicable is being considered voluble, frivolous, fragile, pusillanimous, and irresolute, things that a prince must avoid like an obstacle, striving to show in his actions greatness, courage, gravity, and fortitude; with regard to his private actions with his subjects, he must show that his judgments are irrevocable; he must hold himself to such a concept that no one can think of deceiving or betraying him..

The prince who gives such an impression of himself achieves a good reputation, and the one who is highly esteemed is not easily conspired against. If he is considered an excellent man and revered by his people, he can only be attacked with difficulty.

In fact, a prince must have two fears: one of an internal nature, on the part of his subjects, and the other of an external nature, on the part of foreign potentates. From these, he defends himself with good weapons and good friends; and whenever he has good weapons, he will have good friends. The internal situation, as long as it is not yet disturbed by a conspiracy, will be safe as long as the external situation is stabilized; even when it is disturbed, if the prince organized himself and lived as I have said, as long as he does not become discouraged, he will resist every attack, as I highlighted that Nabis the Spartan did.

But concerning his subjects, when external affairs are not disturbed, he must fear that they will conspire secretly, from which a prince can easily secure himself by avoiding being hated or despised and by keeping the people pleased with him. And this needs to be achieved, as already discussed at length.

One of the most powerful remedies that a prince can have against conspiracies is not to be hated by the majority, because those who conspire always think that with the death of the prince, they will please the people. However, when they consider that this will offend the people, they are not encouraged to take such a course, especially because the difficulties that the conspirators have to face are countless. And as experience shows, there were many conspiracies, but few were successful, because those who conspire cannot act alone, nor can they have as companions other than those they believe to be dissatisfied. But as soon as you have revealed your intention to a dissatisfied person, you give him the material with which to satisfy himself, for by denouncing you, he can look for every advantage; so that, seeing the gain from this course to be assured and seeing the other to be doubtful and full of dangers, he must be a very rare friend, or a thoroughly obstinate enemy of the prince, to keep his word with you.

To reduce the matter to brief terms, I say that on the side of the conspirator, there is nothing but fear, jealousy, and suspicion of punishment to terrify him. But, on the side of the prince, there is the majesty of the principality, the laws, the protection of friends, and the state to defend him, so that, adding to all these things the popular goodwill, it is impossible that anyone should be so reckless as to conspire against the prince. This is because, generally, a conspirator fears the dangers that precede an execution and those that will follow, and if he has the people as his enemy, he must also fear even after the fact has occurred, and therefore cannot expect any support.

Endless examples could be given on this subject; however, I limit myself to just one, preserved by the memory of our parents. Monsignor Annibale Bentivoglio, who was prince in Bologna (and grandfather of the present Monsignor Annibale), was killed by the Canneschi who had conspired against him, with only Monsignor Giovanni left in his family, who was still a child in arms. Shortly after this murder, the people rose up and killed all the Canneschi.

This resulted from the popular prestige that Bentivoglio's house enjoyed in those times. This prestige was so great that, as there was no member of this family left in Bologna capable of ruling the state after Annibale's death, and there was a descendant of the Bentivoglios in Florence who had previously believed himself to be the son of a craftsman, the Bolognese went to that city and entrusted him with the government of that community, which he led until Monsignor Giovanni reached the appropriate age to govern.

I conclude, therefore, that a prince should give little importance to conspiracies if his people hold him in high esteem. But when it is hostile to him and hates him, he must fear everything and everyone. Well-organized states and skillful princes have tried with all diligence not to despair the nobles and to satisfy the people by keeping them happy, especially because this is one of the most important matters that a prince has to deal with.

Among the kingdoms well organized and governed in our time is that of France. In it, there are countless good institutions, on which depend the freedom and security of the king. The first of these is Parliament and its authority. The one who organized this kingdom, knowing the ambition of the nobility and their insolence, deemed it necessary to put a brake in order to correct them, and, on the other hand, knowing the hatred of the majority against the nobles, based on fear, wished to protect them, and did not want all responsibility to fall on the king, exempting him from the hassle of upsetting the nobles by favoring the people and irritating the people by benefiting the nobles. Therefore, he set up a third judge, who should be the one who could beat down the great and favor the lesser without reproach to the king. This order could not be better or more prudent, nor can it be denied that it is the greatest reason for the safety of the king and the kingdom. Hence, another noteworthy conclusion can be drawn: princes must attribute hateful things to others, reserving for themselves those that please them. Again, I conclude that a prince must respect the nobles but not make himself hated by the people.

Considering the life and death of some Roman emperors, perhaps there are examples contrary to my opinion, given that they lived exemplarily and demonstrated great virtues and, despite this, lost the empire or were even killed by those who conspired against them. Therefore, to answer these objections, I will talk about the qualities of some emperors, showing the causes of their ruin, which are not inconsistent with what I said; at the same time, I will take into consideration those facts that are notable for those who read the actions of those times. I consider enough to mention all the emperors who succeeded each other in power, from Marcus, the philosopher, to Maximinus, which were Marcus and his son Commodus, Pertinax, Julian, Severus and his son Antoninus Caracalla, Macrinus, Heliogabalus, Alexander, and Maximinus.

It should be noted initially that, while in other principalities it was enough to fight only against the ambition of the nobles and the insolence of the people, the Roman emperors had a third difficulty in having to endure the cruelty and ambition of the soldiers. This third difficulty was so serious that it became the cause of the ruin of many, as it is difficult to satisfy both the soldiers and the people: the latter loved peace and, therefore, esteemed moderate princes, while the soldiers loved the military-minded prince, who was insolent, cruel, and a thief, wanting him to carry out such violence against the populations so that they could double their pay and vent their greed and cruelty against the people.

Such facts caused those emperors to be always overthrown who, either by birth or training, had no great authority, and most of them, especially those who came new to the principality, recognizing the difficulty of these two opposing humors, were inclined to give satisfaction to the soldiers, caring little about injuring the people. This course was necessary, because, as the prince cannot stop being hated by someone, he must first seek not to be hated by everyone. But when he cannot achieve this, he must endeavor, by all means, to avoid the hatred of those classes that are more powerful. For this reason, those emperors, who, because they were new, needed extraordinary favors, adhered rather to the soldiers than to the people, which, however, became useful or not to them, depending on whether or not they knew how to maintain a reputation among them.

From the reasons mentioned, it resulted that Marcus, Pertinax and Alexander, all of them of modest life, lovers of justice, enemies of cruelty, human and benignant, came to a sad end.

Only Marcus lived and died honored, as he succeeded in the empire by hereditary right, and owed nothing either to the soldiers or the people; later, being endowed with many virtues that made him venerated, he always had, while he lived, one order and another within his limits, never being hated or despised.

But Pertinax, made emperor against the will of the soldiers, who, being accustomed to living licentiously under the empire of Commodus, could not endure the honest life that the emperor wanted to offer. Therefore, Pertinax, having created hatred against himself and adding to it the contempt for being already old, ruined himself at the beginning of his administration.

It should be noted here that hatred is acquired both by good and bad actions. As I said previously, a prince wanting to preserve the state is often forced to not be good because, when that strongest element, be it the people, the soldiers, or the nobles are corrupt, it is better to submit to their desire to satisfy them, so as not to have them against you; then, good works become your enemy.

But let's move on to Alexander, who was a man of such great goodness that, among other praises given to him, there is this one that, in the fourteen years he held power, not a single person was executed without trial; however, being considered fragile and a man who let himself be ruled by his mother, he became despised, the army conspired, and he was killed.

Now talking about, on the other hand, the qualities of Commodus, Severus, Antoninus Caracalla, and Maximinus, we will see that they were all extremely cruel and greedy. To satisfy the soldiers, they did not spare any kind of injury that could be committed against the people; everyone, except Severus, had a sad end. It is because Severus had so much courage that, keeping the soldiers as his friends, even though the people were oppressed by him, he was always able to reign successfully, because his virtues made him so admirable in the opinion of the soldiers and the people, that this was, so to speak, astonished and bewildered, and those respectful and satisfied. And, because his actions were great and remarkable for a new prince, I want to briefly show how well he knew how to use the actions of the fox and the lion, from which natures, as I said before, must be imitated by princes.

Severus, having known the apathy of Emperor Julian, persuaded his army, of which he was captain in Sclavonia, that it was advisable to go to Rome to avenge the death of Pertinax, murdered by Praetorian soldiers; under this pretext, without demonstrating an aspiration for the Empire, he led the army against Rome, arriving in Italy before it was known that he had started. While in Rome, the Senate, out of fear, elected him emperor, and Julian was killed. After this, two difficulties remained for Severus, who wanted to make himself master of the whole empire: one in Asia, where Pescennius Niger, head of the Asian armies, had himself acclaimed emperor; the other in the West, where Albinus was, also aspiring for the empire. Because he considered it dangerous to reveal himself as an enemy of both, he decided to attack Niger and deceive Albinus, to whom he wrote that, having been elected emperor by the Senate, he wanted to share that dignity with him; he sent him the title of Caesar and, by decree of the Senate, made him his colleague. Albinus accepted such things as true. But, after Severus had conquered and killed Niger, having settled eastern affairs, he returned to Rome and complained to the Senate that Albinus, little recognizing the benefits that he had received, had maliciously tried to kill him, and for this ingratitude he was compelled to punish him. Afterward, he went to meet him in France and took away his government and life.

Therefore, whoever examines the actions of this man in detail will realize that he was a very ferocious lion and a very cunning fox, feared and revered by all and not hated by the armies, not surprising that he, a young man, was able to hold so much power; his high reputation always protected him from that hatred that the people might have conceived against him for his violence.

It turns out that Antoninus, his son, was a man who possessed excellent qualities that made him wonderful in the people's opinion and beloved by the soldiers; he was a military man who endured any fatigue very well, despised delicate foods and other luxuries, which made him loved by all the armies. However, his ferocity and cruelty were so great and unprecedented that, after endless single murders, he killed a large number of the population of Rome and the entire population of Alexandria. He became hated by the whole world, and also feared by those he had around him, to such an extent that he was killed by a centurion in the midst of his army.

THE PRINCE

In connection with the above, it should be noted that such murders, resulting from the deliberation of an obstinate spirit, cannot be avoided by princes, because anyone who is not afraid of dying can strike them. However, the prince has little to fear, because such deaths are rare. He must only take care not to cause serious injury to any of those he employs and has around him in the service of the principality, as Antoninus did, who had vilely murdered one of that centurion's brothers and also threatened him daily, while he kept him in his own guard; this resolution was reckless and capable of destroying him, as happened.

Let's move on to Commodus, for whom it was very easy to maintain the empire by possessing it by inheritance, since he was the son of Marcus. All he had to do was follow in his father's footsteps, and he would have satisfied the soldiers and the people. But being of a cruel and brutal nature, in order to use his trickery against the people, he started captivating the armies, making them licentious; on the other hand, by not maintaining his dignity, frequently descending to the arenas to fight with gladiators, doing other extremely vile things and little worthy of the imperial majesty, he became despicable in the opinion of the soldiers. And being hated by some and despised by others, they conspired against him, and he was killed.

It remains for us to narrate the qualities of Maximinus. He was a very warlike man, and the armies, being disgusted with the effeminacy of Alexander, of whom I have already spoken, killed him and elected Maximinus to the government. Maximinus did not stay in power for long, as two things made him hated and despised: one, the fact that he came from an extremely humble origin, having herded sheep in Thrace (a fact well known to everyone and which caused him great depreciation in the general concept); the other, because, having delayed at the beginning of his principality in going to Rome and taking possession of the imperial throne; he had also gained a reputation for the utmost ferocity by having, through his prefects in Rome and elsewhere in the empire, practiced many cruelties. So that the whole world was moved to anger at the meanness of his blood and filled with hatred by fear of his ferocity, Africa rebelled first, then the Senate with all the people of Rome. That is when all of Italy conspired against him. His own army joined this movement, campaigning in Aquileia and finding it difficult to siege, disgusted by his cruelty, fearing him less for seeing him with so many enemies, killed him.

I do not want to talk about Heliogabalus, Macrinus, or Julian, who, because they were entirely despicable, were quickly wiped out. I will therefore proceed to the conclusion of this matter. Thus, I say that the princes of our times have much less difficulty satisfying their soldiers, because, although some consideration must be given to them, this is quickly resolved, as none of these princes have an army that is a veteran in the governments and administrations of the provinces, as were the armies of the Roman Empire. However, if it was then more necessary to give satisfaction to the soldiers than to the people, it is now more necessary for all princes, except the Turk and the Soldan, to satisfy the people rather than the soldiers, because the people are more powerful.

I make an exception for the Turk because he always has twelve thousand infantry and fifteen thousand cavalry soldiers around him, on which depend the security and power of his kingdom. And it is necessary that, putting aside every consideration for the people, he should keep them his friends. You must note that this kingdom of the Soldan is different from all other principalities: it is similar to the Christian pontificate, which cannot be called either a hereditary principality or a new principality since it is not the children of the old prince who inherit and become lords, but rather the one elected to the position by those who have authority. And, as this is an old custom, it cannot be called a new principality, because there are none of those difficulties in it that are met with in new ones; for although the prince is new, the constitution of the state is old, and it is framed so as to receive him as if he was its hereditary lord.

> *"Princes must attribute hateful things to others, reserving for themselves those that please them."*

Let's return, however, to our subject. I say that anyone who considers the above will see that hatred or contempt was the cause of the ruin of the emperors mentioned and will also know why, if one part of them acted in one way and the other part in the opposite way, in any of these ways of acting, some of them ended happily while others ended unhappily.

For Pertinax and Alexander, as they were new princes, it was useless and harmful to try to imitate Marcus, who was in a principality of hereditary origin. Likewise, it was pernicious for Caracalla, Commodus, and Maximinus to imitate Severus, as they did not possess enough virtue for them to be able to follow his footsteps.

Therefore, a new prince, in a new principality, cannot imitate the actions of Marcus, and it is also not necessary to follow the actions of Severus. However, he must take from Severus those qualities that are necessary to found his state, and from Marcus those that are convenient and glorious to maintain a government already established and firm.

Chapter XX
Whether fortresses and many other things made by princes are useful or not
(An arces et multa alia quae cotidie a principibus fiunt utilia an inutilia sint)

In order to securely maintain the state, some princes disarmed their subjects, others kept the subject lands divided, some fostered enmities against themselves, others dedicated themselves to gaining the support of those who were suspicious of them at the beginning of their government, some built fortresses, others ruined and destroyed them. And, although it is not possible to establish a certain judgment on all these things without going into the particularities of each of the states where some of these deliberations should be taken, I will speak in a generic way compatible with the matter.

There was never a new prince who disarmed his subjects, but, before, whenever he found them disarmed, he armed them; this is because, by arming them, these weapons become yours, those men who were distrusted become faithful, and those who were faithful are kept so, and your subjects become your supporters. And because all subjects cannot be armed, those you arm are benefited and you can deal with others more safely; this diversity in their treatment that they recognize in your favor makes them obligated towards you, and others will excuse you, believing it is necessary for those to have more rewards for being subjected to greater dangers and greater obligations. But when you disarm them, you begin to offend them by showing that you doubt them, either out of vileness or distrust. One or another of these opinions conceives hatred against you. And, because you cannot remain unarmed, it becomes necessary for you to turn to the mercenary militia, which is of a quality that has already been said, and even if it was good, it would not be enough to defend you against powerful enemies and distrusted subjects.

However, a new prince in a new principality always organized the armed forces, and history is full of these examples. But, when a prince conquers a new state, which he adds as a province to his old one, then it is necessary to disarm the conquered state, except those that were your supporters in the conquest; and even these, with time and opportunity, it will be necessary to make them docile and meek, proceeding in such a way that the weapons are only in the possession of your own soldiers, those who, in the old state, were with you.

Our ancestors and those who were considered wise used to say that Pistoia needed to be maintained by dividing the people and Pisa by fortresses. For this reason, in some regions they conquered, they maintained disagreements between the parties to control them more easily. This, in those times when Italy had a certain balance, must have been useful. But I do not believe that this can be accepted as a current precept, as I do not believe that divisions could ever bring any benefit; on the contrary, when the enemy approaches, the divided cities are necessarily quickly lost, because the weakest part will always join the external forces and the other will not be able to resist.

The Venetians, driven by the reasons already mentioned, I believe, encouraged the Guelph and Ghibelline factions in the cities subject to them; and, although they never allowed them to fight, they fed these differences between them so that, once the citizens were distracted by their differences, they would not unite against them. This, as we saw, did not bring them any benefit because, defeated in Vaila, some of those cities soon began to rise up and take the entire state from them.

Such attitudes reveal a weakness in the prince, because similar divisions will never be allowed in a powerful principality. Such attitudes are useful only in times of peace because through them, it is possible to manage subjects more easily; but when war comes, such a system demonstrates its fallacy.

Without a doubt, princes become great when they overcome the difficulties and oppositions placed before them; however, fortune, especially when it wants to make a new prince great, who has more need to acquire a reputation than a hereditary one, causes enemies to arise and determines that they be faced, so that he has the opportunity to overcome them and thus be able to climb higher up the ladder that the enemies offer him. For this reason, many think that a skillful prince should, when he has the opportunity, cunningly encourage some enmity so that, once this is eliminated, he can continue the rise of his greatness.

Princes, especially new ones, have found more loyalty and greater usefulness in men who, at the beginning of their government, were considered suspects, than in those who were initially their confidants. Pandolfo Petrucci, Prince of Siena, ruled his state more with those who had been distrusted than with others.

It is not possible to talk about this question in a generic way, as it varies according to each case. I will only say this: the men who at the beginning of a principality had been enemies, in a condition that, in order to maintain themselves need support, the prince will always be able to conquer them with great ease, and they will be tightly forced to serve the prince with loyalty, inasmuch as they recognize that it is necessary for them to cancel by works the bad impression that he had formed of them.

Thus, the prince always extracts more profit from those who, serving him with excessive security, may neglect his interests.

Since the matter demands it, I do not want to fail to remind the princes that took over a new state by means of the favor of some of the inhabitants of the same state, that they must consider well the reason that determined those who favored him to act in this way; if this is not natural affection towards them, but rather if the support resulted from the fact that they were not satisfied with the former state, only with fatigue and great difficulty will the prince be able to keep them friends, given that it is almost impossible that they can be satisfied.

Considering carefully the examples that can be drawn from ancient and modern things, as a result of this, it will be seen that it is much easier for the prince to make friends with those men who were satisfied with the old regime and, therefore, were his enemies, than with those who, out of discontent, became his friends and favored him in the conquest.

It has been the custom of princes, in order to maintain their state more securely, to build fortresses that serve as a rein and brake to those who want to confront them, as well as a safe refuge against a surprise attack. I praise this procedure because it has been used since ancient times. However, Monsignor Nicollò Vitelli, in modern times, destroyed two fortresses in the City of Castello in order to preserve the state. Guido Ubaldo, Duke of Urbino, having returned to his domain from which he had been expelled by Cesare Borgia, destroyed to the foundations all the fortresses in that province, understanding that without them it would be more difficult to lose his state again. The Bentivoglios returned to Bologna and used the same method. Therefore, fortresses are useful or not, according to the circumstances; if they do you good on the one hand, they harm you on the other. This statement can be explained in the following way.

The prince who fears his people more than foreigners must build fortresses, but whoever is more afraid of foreigners than of his own people must abandon them. The castle of Milan, built by Francisco Sforza, made and will make more war for the Sforza house than any other disorder in that state.

For this reason, the best fortress that can exist is not being hated by the people. Even if you have fortifications, they are worthless if the people hate you, and once the people take up weapons, there is never a lack of foreigners to support them.

In our times, it is clear that fortresses have not been beneficial to any prince, except for the Countess of Forli. When Count Girolamo, her husband, died, she, taking refuge in a fortification, was able to escape the popular attack, wait for help from Milan, and recover the state; furthermore, the circumstances were such that a foreigner could not help the people.

Later, the fortresses were also of little use to her when Cesare Borgia attacked her and when the people, her enemy, allied themselves with the foreigner. Therefore, it would have been safer for her not to be hated by the people than to have fortresses. Considering all these questions, I will praise both those who build and those who do not build fortresses and I will blame anyone who, trusting in fortifications, cares little about being hated by the people.

CHAPTER XXI
What is Appropriate to a Prince to be Esteemed For
(Quod principem deceat ut egregius habeatur)

Nothing makes a prince as esteemed as great undertakings and setting a fine example. In our time, we can mention Ferdinand of Aragon, the present King of Spain. This one can be called a new prince because from a weak king, he became, through fame and glory, the first king of Christians, and if you consider his actions, you will find them all great and some even extraordinary.

At the beginning of his reign, he occupied Granada, and this undertaking was the foundation of his state. First, he did it alone, without fighting with other states and without fear of being prevented from doing so; he kept the attention of the barons of Castile occupied in this venture, who, thinking about the war, did not consider innovations; and he, through this means, acquired reputation and authority over them without their realizing it. He was able to maintain his armies with money from the Church and the people, and with such a long campaign, he established the organization of his militia that later brought him so much honor.

Furthermore, in order to establish greater undertakings, always using religion, Aragon dedicated himself to merciful cruelty, expelling and ridding his kingdom of the Moors, an action of which there can be no more miserable or more admirable example. Under this same cover, he attacked Africa, campaigned in Italy, and conquered France; thus, he always made and devised great undertakings, which at all times kept the minds of his subjects in suspense and admiration, busy waiting for the success of these wars. And his actions have arisen in such a way, one out of the other, that men have never been given time to work steadily against him.

It is a great pleasure for a prince to give memorable examples of himself in the way he behaves towards his subjects, similar to those narrated by Monsignor Bernabo of Milan, when the opportunity arises for someone to have accomplished something extraordinary, good or bad, in civil life, obtaining means of rewarding or punishing him in a way that is widely commented upon. Above all, a prince must strive to give of himself, in every action, the concept of a great man and of extraordinary intelligence.

A prince is also esteemed when he is a true friend or enemy, that is, when, without any consideration, he reveals himself in favor of one against another one. This attitude is always more useful than remaining neutral because, if two of your powerful neighbors get into a fight, they are of such a character that, if one of them conquers, you have either to fear him or not.

In either of these two cases, it will always be more useful to define yourself and fight a worthy war, because in the first case, if you do not define yourself, you will invariably fall prey to the conqueror, to the pleasure and satisfaction of the one who has been conquered, and you will have no reasons to offer, nor anything to protect or shelter you. Because the one who conquers does not want doubtful friends who will not help him in adversity; and the one who loses will not welcome you because you did not willingly, sword in hand, court his fate.

Antiochus invaded Greece at the call of the Aetolians to expel the Romans. He sent ambassadors to the Achaeans, friends of the Romans, to urge them to remain neutral, while the Romans persuaded them to take up weapons on their side. This matter came to the deliberation of the Achaeans congress, where the legacy of Antiochus induced them to neutrality; to this, the Roman representative answered: *Quod autem isti dicunt non interponendi vos bello, nihil magis alienum rebus vestris est; sine gratia, sine dignitate, praemium victoris eritis*. ("As for the opinion that you should not interfere in the war, it is the most unfavorable decision you could make: deprived of credit and dignity, you will be a prize for the conqueror").

It will always happen that the one who is not a friend will seek your neutrality, and the one who is a friend will ask you to define yourself with weapons. Irresolute princes, to escape present dangers, most often follow the path of neutrality and generally fall into ruin. But, when a prince defines himself gallantly in favor of one side, if the one with whom he allies himself conquers, even if the conqueror is so powerful and may have him at his mercy, he has an obligation towards him, and there is established a bond of friendship, and men are never so shameless as to become a monument of ingratitude by oppressing you.

Furthermore, victories are never so brilliant that the winner should have no regard, especially for what is fair. But if the one with whom you ally yourself loses, you will be supported by him, and as long as he can, he will help you, and you will be associated with a fortune that could rise again. In the second case, when those who fight are of a class that should not fear the conqueror, even greater prudence is to be allied, as it causes the ruin of one with the help of those who should save him if he was wise; if he wins, he is at your mercy, and it is impossible for him not to win with your help.

A prince must be careful never to make an alliance with someone more powerful than himself to attack others, unless necessity compels him, as I said above, because if he conquers you, you are at his discretion, and princes must escape as much as possible from being at the discretion of anyone.

The Venetians allied themselves with France against the Duke of Milan, and this alliance, which caused their ruin, could have been avoided. But, when it cannot be avoided (as happened to the Florentines when the Pope and Spain led their armies to attack Lombardy), then the prince must favor one of the sides for the reasons explained above. Never let any state imagine that it can choose perfectly safe sides; rather, let it expect to have to take very doubtful ones; it is seen in the order of things that one never seeks to escape one inconvenience without incurring another one, and prudence consists in knowing the nature of these inconveniences and taking the least harmful as a good one.

A prince must also show himself to be a lover of virtue, giving opportunities to virtuous men and honoring the best in every art. At the same time, he must encourage its citizens to peacefully carry out their activities in commerce, agriculture, and any other occupation, so that the farmer does not fear decorating his properties for fear that they will be taken from him, while the trader must not stop carrying out his trade for fear of fees; he must, furthermore, establish prizes for those who want to accomplish such things and those who think of enhancing their city or state in any way. In addition, at convenient times of the year, he should entertain the people with parties and spectacles.

Since every city is divided into art guilds or social groups, he must take care of these guilds and groups, meet with them sometimes, and give proof of humanity and munificence, always maintaining, nevertheless, the majesty of his dignity. For this, he must never be lacking in anything.

CHAPTER XXII
Concerning the Secretaries that Princes Have with Them
(De his quos a secretis principes habent)

It is of no small importance to a prince the choice of ministers, whether they are good or not, according to the prudence of the prince himself. And the first conjecture that is made about a master's intelligence results

THE PRINCE

from the observation of the men around him; when they are capable and faithful, he may always be considered wise because he knew how to recognize them as capable and to keep them faithful. But when they are not like that, one can always make a bad judgment about the prince, because the first mistake he makes lies in that choice.

There was no one, knowing Monsignor Antonio de Venafro as a minister of Pandolfo Petrucci, Prince of Siena, who would not consider Pandolfo as extremely valuable for having him as a minister. And because intelligent men are of three kinds: the one who understands things by himself, the one who discerns what others understand, and the one who understands neither by himself nor by others. The first is excellent, the second is very good, and the third is useless. It was inevitable, therefore, that if Pandolfo was not classified in the first degree, he would necessarily be in the second, because every time someone has the ability to know the good and evil that a person does or says, even if he does not have the ability to solve the problems himself, he discerns the bad and good works of the minister, praises these, and corrects those, and the minister cannot hope to deceive him, so he remains honest.

However, for a prince to meet the minister, there is a method that does not fail: when you see the minister thinking more about himself than about you, and that in all his actions he seeks his own interest, you can conclude that he will never be a good minister, and you will never be able to trust him; the one who has the state of others in his hands should never think of himself, but always of his prince, and never consider things that do not concern only to him. On the other hand, for the prince to retain a good minister, he must think about him, honor him, make him rich, and make him participate in honors and positions, so that he sees that he cannot be without his protection and that the many honors do not make him desire more honors, the many riches do not make him desire greater riches and the many positions make him fear changes. When, therefore, ministers, and princes with respect to them, are thus prepared, they can trust one another; when this is not the case, the end will always be harmful to one or the other.

CHAPTER XXIII
How flatterers should be avoided
(Quomodo adulatores sint fugiendi)

I do not want to leave out an important point, a mistake from which princes can only defend themselves with great difficulty if they are not extremely prudent or if they do not make a good choice. I am talking about the flatterers, of whom the courts are full, given that men take so much pleasure in their own affairs and deceive themselves in such a way that it is difficult for them to defend themselves from this pest, and, in wanting to defend themselves, there is the danger of becoming belittled. Because there is no other way of guarding oneself from flatterers except by making men understand that they do not offend you by telling the truth, but when everyone can tell you the truth, they start to lack reverence.

Therefore, a wise prince must proceed in a third way, choosing wise men in his state, and only to them should he give the freedom to tell him the truth of what he asks and nothing more. But he must consult them about all matters and listen to their opinions; then, decide for himself, in his own way, and, with this advice and with each one of them, behave in such a way that everyone understands that the more freely they speak, the more easily their opinions will be accepted. Apart from those, he should listen to no one, follow the deliberation adopted, and be obstinate in his decisions. Whoever does otherwise is either overthrown by flatterers or is so often changed by varying opinions that he falls into contempt.

In this regard, I would like to provide a current example. Fra Luca, man of the present Emperor Maximilian, speaking of His Majesty, said that he did not take advice from anyone and did nothing in his own way; this resulted from having a custom contrary to the above. Because the Emperor is a discreet man, and he does not communicate his designs to anyone; he does not ask for opinions; but, as in carrying them into effect they become revealed and known, and they begin to be contradicted by those around him, and he, as a man of weak opinion, undoes them. It turns out that the things he does one day he undoes the next, and no one ever understands what he wants or intends to do, and no one can rely on his resolutions.

A prince, therefore, must always take advice, but only when he wants to and not when others want to; rather, he must discourage everyone from offering advice unless he asks for it. But he must be a great inquirer and then, regarding the things asked, a patient listener of the truth; also, noticing that someone, on any consideration, did not tell him the truth, he should let his anger be felt.

There are many who understand that a prince who gives an impression of his wisdom is considered not because of his nature, but because of the good advisers that surround him; however, without a doubt, they are deceived, because this is a general rule that never fails: a prince who is not wise in himself will never take good advice unless by chance he has yielded his affairs entirely to one person who happens to be a very prudent man. In this case, indeed, he may be well governed, but it would not be for long, because such a governor, in a short time, would take away his state from him. But if a prince who is not wise should take advice from more than one, he will never get united advice and will not know how to unite them.

Each counselor will think for himself, and he will not know how to correct them or find out about the matter. And it is not possible to find different counselors, because men will always be untrue if they are not made honest by necessity. Consequently, it follows that good advice, wherever it comes from, must arise from the wisdom of the prince, and not the wisdom of the prince from good advice.

CHAPTER XXIV
WHY DID THE PRINCES OF ITALY LOSE THEIR STATES?

(Cur Italiae principes regnum amiserunt)

The things already mentioned, carefully observed, will enable a new prince to appear well established and render him at once more secure and fixed in the state than if he had been long seated there.

Because a new prince is much more observed in his actions than a hereditary one, and when these actions are recognized as virtuous, they attract men more strongly and bind them to themselves much more than the tradition of blood.

Because men are more attracted by present things than by past things, and when they find good in the present ones, they are satisfied and look for nothing else. Rather, they will assume all his defense, as long as he does not break his word in other matters. Thus, it will be a double glory for him to have established a new principality and strengthened it with good laws, good weapons, and good examples; on the other hand, for the one who, having been born a prince lost the state due to his lack of prudence, it will be a double shame.

And, when considering those lords who, in Italy, have lost their states in our times, such as the King of Naples, the Duke of Milan, and others, one will find in them, first, a common defect regarding weapons, for the reasons that have already been exposed; later, it will be seen that some of them, either had the enmity of the people or, having the people as their friend, did not know how to protect themselves against the nobles; without these defects, states have power enough to keep an army in the field and cannot be lost. Philip of Macedonia, not the father of Alexander the Great, but the one who was defeated by Titus Quintius, had a state that was not very extensive, compared to the greatness of the Romans and Greece that attacked him; however, because he was a man with a military spirit, who knew how to have the people as friends and protect himself against the nobles, he maintained the war against his enemies for many years; and if, after all, he lost control of some cities, he was left with the kingdom.

> *"A wise prince must proceed in a third way, choosing wise men in his state and only to them he should give the freedom to tell him the truth of what he asks and nothing more."*

Therefore, do not let our princes accuse fortune for the loss of their principalities after so many years' possession, but rather their own sloth, because in quiet times they never thought there could be a change (which is a common defect of men in good times not to worry about the storm) and when afterward the bad times came, they worried about fleeing and not defending themselves, hoping that the populations, tired of the insolence of the conquerors, would call them back. This option is good when others fail, but it is very bad to abandon other courses for this one, as you will not fall just because you believe you will find someone to lift you; it does not happen or, if it does, it will not be for your safety, since that defense becomes vile if it does not depend on you. Defenses are only good, reliable, and lasting when they depend on yourself and your virtue.

CHAPTER XXV
HOW MUCH CAN FORTUNE AFFECT IN HUMAN AFFAIRS AND HOW CAN IT BE WITHSTOOD?

(Quantum fortuna in rebus humanis possit,
et quomodo illi sit occurren dum)

I am not unaware that many have the opinion that the things of the world are governed by fortune and by God, in a way that men, with their wisdom, cannot modify or avoid them in any way; therefore, one might think that it is not advisable to insist too much on things but rather to let oneself be governed by fortune.

This opinion has become more accepted in our times due to the great changes in things that are observed every day, regardless of any human conjecture. After thinking about it a few times, I am partly inclined in favor of this opinion. However, so that our free will is not extinguished, I think it may be true that fortune is the arbiter of half of our actions, but that it still leaves us to govern the other half, or perhaps a little less. I compare it to one of those torrential rivers that, when they rage, flood the plains, destroy trees and buildings, and bear away the earth from one place to another; everyone flees before it, and everything gives way to its violence, without being able to withstand it anyway. And, if this happened, it would not prevent men, when the times were calm, from taking measures with defenses and barriers in such a manner that, rising again, either the waters would flow through a channel, or their force would not be so unrestrained and not so harmful.

The same happens with fortune, which shows its power where there is no virtue prepared to withstand it and then, turns its forces towards the point where defenses and barriers were not built to restrain it. And, if you consider Italy, which is the seat of these variations and the one that gave rise to them, you will see that it is a region without barriers and any defense, as it was protected by convenient military forces, like Germany, Spain, and France, either this overflow would not have made the great changes it did, or it would not have occurred. I think it is concerning enough what I had to say about the opposition that can be faced against fortune in general. But, restricting myself more to the particular, I say why one sees a prince today in clear and happy progress and tomorrow in ruin, without having changed his nature or his qualities. This results, as I believe, firstly from the reasons that were explained at length above, that is, that the prince who relies entirely on fortune falls into disgrace when it changes.

I also believe it is happy the one who adapts his way of acting to the nature of the times, in the same way that I think it is unhappy the one who, with his behavior, comes into conflict with the moment he is going through. Because men are seen in affairs that take them to the end that each one has as their objective, that is, glories and riches, proceeding in different ways: one with caution, another with haste; one with violence, another with cunning; one with patience, another in the opposite way; and each one, by these different means, can reach the goal.

It is also seen, of two cautious men, one reaching his goal and the other not, and in the same way, two of them equally reach a happy end with two different tendencies, being, for example, one cautious and the other impetuous; all this arises from nothing else than whether or not they conform in their methods to the spirit of the times. This results from what I said, that is, that two men, acting in different ways, can achieve the same effect, while of two working equally, one achieves his goal and the other one does not.

The variation in the concept of good also depends on this, because if someone guides himself with caution and patience, times and situations present themselves in such a way that his guidance is good, and he achieves happiness. But if times and circumstances change, he falls into disgrace, as he has not changed his way of acting. But a man is not often found sufficiently circumspect to know how to accommodate himself to the change, either because he cannot deviate from what nature inclines him to or because, if he has prospered by always following a path, he cannot leave it.

Therefore, the cautious man, when it is time to turn adventurous, does not know how to do it and, as a result, falls into ruin, since if he changed his nature according to times and things, his fortune would not change.

Pope Julius II, in all his affairs, proceeded impetuously and found both times and circumstances coinciding with his way of proceeding, so he always achieved happy success. Consider his first campaign against Bologna, while Monsignor Giovanni Bentivoglio was still alive.

The Venetians were discontented; the King of Spain, under the same conditions – he still discussed his campaign with France. Nevertheless, he personally entered upon the expedition with his accustomed boldness and energy, a move which made Spain and the Venetians stand irresolute and passive, the latter from fear, the former from desire to recover the entire kingdom of Naples; on the other hand, he dragged with him the King of France, because that king, having observed him on campaign and wanting to make him his friend in order to debase the Venetians, thought he could not deny him his people without insulting him in a clear way.

Pope Julius II accomplished, therefore, with his impetuous movement, what no other pontiff, with all human wisdom, would ever have done, because if he, to leave Rome, had expected to have all the plans established and all the settled things, as any other pope would have done, would never have been successful. In fact, the King of France would have made a thousand excuses and others would have instilled a thousand fears in him. I want to omit his other actions, all similar and all successful, since the brevity of his life did not allow him to experience the opposite, because if times had come when it had become necessary to act with caution, his ruin would certainly have come, because he would never have deviated from that way of proceeding to which nature inclined him.

I conclude, therefore, that fortune can be changeful, and men can remain obstinate in their ways of acting, so, they will be happy as long as the two are in agreement and unhappy when disagreement arises. I consider that it is better to be impetuous than cautious, because fortune is a woman and consequently becomes necessary, wanting to dominate, beat, and contradict her; and she allows herself to be defeated more by these than by those who act coldly. Fortune, however, like a woman, is always a friend of young people, because they are less cautious, more daring, and with greater audacity, they dominate her.

CHAPTER XXVI
AN EXHORTATION TO TAKE ITALY AND FREE IT FROM THE HANDS OF THE BARBARIANS

(Exhortatio ad capessendam italiam in libertatemque a barbaris vindicandam)

Considering, then, all the things already explained, I thought to myself whether at the present moment, in Italy, there were times capable of honoring a new prince and whether there was material that would assure someone, wise and brave, the opportunity to introduce a new organization that would bring him honor and do good for all the people. It seems to me that there are so many circumstances favorable to a new prince that I never knew a time more fit than the present. And if, as I said, to know the virtue of Moses it was necessary that the people of Israel were enslaved in Egypt; to know the greatness of the soul of Cyrus, the Persians were oppressed by the Medes; and to know the value of Theseus, that the

Athenians were dispersed, also in the present, wanting to know the virtue of an Italian spirit, it would be necessary for Italy to reduce itself to the point in which it finds itself at the moment, for it to be more enslaved than the Hebrews, more oppressed than the Persians, more disunited than the Athenians, without a leader, without order, beaten, plundered lacerated, invaded, and had endured ruin of all sorts.

If a certain glimpse of hope appeared regarding some prince sent from God for the redemption of Italy, however, it was later seen that the apogee of his actions was abandoned by fortune. So, with Italy rendered lifeless, it waits for someone to heal its wounds and put an end to the looting of Lombardy, the killings in the kingdom of Naples and Tuscany, and clean those sores that for long have festered. It is seen how it begs God to send someone to redeem it from these barbaric cruelties and insolence. It is also seen that it is all ready and willing to follow a flag, as long as there is someone to carry it.

Neither is it seen at present as the one it can trust other than his illustrious house, which, with his fortune and virtue, favored by God and the Church, of which he is now prince, will be able to become the head of this redemption. This will not be very difficult if he tries to follow the actions and lives of those mentioned. And, although those men were rare and wonderful, they were men nonetheless, and all of them had less opportunity than the present offers: because their undertakings were neither fairer nor easier than this, nor was God more friendly to them.

What I say is very fair: *justum enim est bellum quibus necessarium, et pia arma ubi nulla nisi in armis spes est* (because fair is war when necessary, and merciful are weapons when there is no hope left but in them).

Here there is a great willingness, and where this exists, there can be no great difficulty, as long as one imitates the way of acting of those I pointed out as an example. In addition, here we see extraordinary events emanating from God: the sea opened, a cloud revealed the way, the stone poured water, and it rained manna; all things contributed to your greatness. The rest must be done by you. God does not want to do everything, so as not to take away our free will and part of that glory that belongs to us.

And it is no wonder if any of the aforementioned Italians have not been able to do what is expected from their illustrious house, and if, in so many Italian revolutions and in so many war campaigns, it always seems that in this, military virtue is extinct. This results from the fact that their old institutions were not good and there was no one who knew how to find others; and nothing does so much honor to a new prince as new laws and new regulations drawn up by him. These, when they are well-founded and dignified, make the prince worthy of reverence and admiration, and in Italy there are not wanting opportunities to bring such into use in every form. Here there is great value in the people, while it is lacking in the leaders.

I observed in duels and individual combats how superior the Italians are in strength, dexterity, or ingenuity. But when it comes to the armies, they do not bear comparison. And everything results from the weakness of the leaders, because those who are capable are not obedient, and each one seems to know, so far, no one has emerged who has known how to excel by virtue or fortune in such a way that others give in. Hence, it is that, in so many years, in so many wars over the last twenty years, whenever an entirely Italian army was formed, it set a bad example, as demonstrated by Taro, then Alexandria, Capua, Genoa, Vailà, Bologna, Mestri.

If, therefore, your illustrious house wants to follow those excellent men and redeem your provinces, it is necessary, before anything else, as the true foundation of any undertaking, to provide yourself with your own troops, because there can be no more faithful, truer, or better soldiers. And, although each of them is good, all of them together will become even better, when they see themselves commanded by their prince and honored and maintained by him. It is therefore necessary to prepare these armies to be able, with Italian virtue, to defend themselves against foreigners.

And, although the Swiss and Spanish infantry may be considered formidable, there are defects in both, so a third type of infantry could not only oppose them but also be able to overcome them.

Because the Spanish cannot face the cavalry and the Swiss must be afraid of the infantry when in combat, they find them as obstinate as they are. It has already been seen, and still is seen, that the Spanish could not face a French cavalry and the Swiss were defeated by a Spanish infantry.

And although complete proof of this latter cannot be shown, nevertheless there was some evidence of it at the campaign of Ravenna when the Spanish infantries faced German battalions, which had the same organization as the Swiss; when the Spanish, with the agility of their bodies and the help of their small shields, got in under the pikes of the Germans and were certain of injuring and killing them without them being able to prevent it; in fact, if it was not for the cavalry that attacked them, they would have eliminated all the enemies.

It is possible, therefore, knowing the defect of both these infantries, to organize a different one that resists the cavalry and is not afraid of the infantry, which will give superior quality to the armies and impose a change in tactics. These are those things that, when reformed, give reputation and greatness to a new prince.

Therefore, this opportunity should not be allowed to pass, so that Italy, after so long, can meet its redeemer. Nor can I express with what love he would be received in all those provinces that have suffered from these foreign invasions, with what thirst for revenge, with what obstinate faith, with what mercy, with what tears. What doors would be closed to him? Which people would deny him obedience? What envy would oppose him? Which Italian would deny him its favor? This barbaric domain is disgusting to everyone. Let, therefore, your illustrious house take up this task with that spirit and with that hope with which fair causes are embraced, so that, under its banner, this country may be liberated and under its auspices may be verified that saying of Petrarch:

Virtù contro a furore
Prenderà l'arme, e fia el combatter corto;
Ché l'antico valore
Nell'italici cor non è ancor morto.
(Virtue against fury shall advance the fight,
And it in combat will soon put to flight,
For the old Roman valor is not dead,
As it lives on in Italian hearts.)

NICCOLÒ MACHIAVELLI

LETTER TO FRANCESCO VETTORI
To the magnificent Florentine orator, Francesco Vettori,
before the Supreme Pontiff and his benefactor
(Magnificooratori Florentino Francisco Vectoriapud
Summum Pontificem et benefactori suo)

Magnificent ambassador,
"Divine graces were never late." I say this because it seemed to me that your grace had not lost, but rather had faded, as you had not written to me for a long time; I was in doubt about what the reason might be. And I gave little importance to all those reasons that came to my mind, except when I thought that you had ceased writing to me, because it had been written to you that I was not a good guardian of your letters; and I knew that, except for Filippo and Pagolo, others, for my part, had not seen them. I am reassured by your recent letter of the 23rd of last month, from which I am extremely pleased to see how orderly and calmly you exercise this public function, and I encourage you to continue in this manner, because whoever leaves his comforts for the comforts of others, loses his own and gets no gratitude from them. Since fortune wants to arrange all things, it is necessary to let it do it, remain quiet, and not create embarrassment, waiting for time to allow it to do something for men. Then, it will be good for you to persevere more unfailingly, to be more alert about matters, and for me to leave the village and say: "Here I am." I cannot, therefore, wanting to render your equal graces, say anything in this letter of mine other than what my life is, and if you think it is worth exchanging it with yours, I will be happy to make the exchange.

Here I am, in the village, and since my latest disasters, I have not spent a total of twenty days in Florence. Until now, I have been catching robins with my own hands. I got up before dawn, prepared the trap, went beyond with a bundle of birdcages on my shoulder. I looked like Geta when he returned from the harbor with Amphitryon's books; I caught at least two and at most six robins. And so, I spent the entire month of November. Afterward, this diversion, although despicable and strange, came to an end – to my regret. I *will describe what my life is now. I get up in the morning with the sun and go to the woods that I am having cut down; there I spend a couple of hours inspecting the work of the previous day and spending time with the woodsmen who are always having some trouble with each other or with their neighbors. I could tell you a thousand good stories about these woods and my experiences with them, as well as about Frosino da Panzano and the others who wanted this firewood. Frosino, in particular, sent for a certain amount without telling me anything and, at the time of payment, he wanted to withhold ten lire that he said he had won from me, four years ago, when he had beaten me at a cricca game at Antonio Guicciardini's house. I started to raise hell: I wanted to accuse the wagoner, who had been sent there by him, as a thief, but Giovanni Machiavelli intervened and put us in agreement. Batista Guicciardini, Filippo Ginori, Tommaso dei Bene, and some other citizens, when the north wind started blowing, all ordered a pile of firewood from me. I promised some to each one; I sent Tommaso a load, which arrived in Florence in half, because, to pile it up, there were he, his wife, his children, and the servants, which looked like Gabburra when on Thursday, with his boys, slaughtered an ox. So, seeing who I was depositing my earnings with, I told the others that I had no more wood; everyone was angry about it, especially Battista, who included this among the other misfortunes of Prato.*

Leaving the woods, I go to a spring and, from there, to my robin nursery. I have a book under my arm: Dante, Petrarch, or one of the minor poets like Tibullus, Ovid, or some such. I read about their loving passions, and their loves remind me of mine, and these reflections make me happy for a while. Then I make my way along the road toward the inn; I talk to passersby, ask for news about their cities, I hear many things and notice different tastes and fantasies of men. Meanwhile, lunchtime arrives, when with my family I eat the foods that this poor village and this small heritage yield. After lunch, I return to the inn; here, generally, are the innkeeper, a butcher, a miller and two bakers. With these, I debase myself all day long playing cricca and trichtach: these games lead to thousands of squabbles and endless incidents with insulting words. More often than not, we are wrangling over a penny; be that as it may, people can hear us yelling even in San Casciano. Thus, having been cooped up among these lice, I get the mold out of my brain and let out the malice of my fate, being happy if you would meet me on this road to discover whether or not my fate is ashamed of treating me so.

When evening comes, I return home and enter my office; at the door, I take off my workday clothes, covered with clay and mud, and put on clothes worthy of a king and the court and, dressed like this, I enter the ancient courts of the men of the past, where, received kindly by them, I nourish myself with that food that is uniquely mine, for which I was born; I am not ashamed to talk to them and ask them the reasons for their actions. And they, out of their human kindness, answer me. And for four hours, I do not feel any boredom, I forget all my afflictions, I do not fear poverty, I am not afraid of death: I integrate myself entirely with them. And, because Dante said that no one understands anything unless it retains what it has understood, I wrote down what I made capital of through his conversation, and composed a short study, De Principatibus, in which I delve as deeply as I can into the ideas concerning this topic, discussing the definition of principality, the categories of principalities, how they are acquired, how they are maintained, and why they are lost. If you have ever pleased any of my fantasies, this one should not displease you; and a prince, especially a new prince, should accept this work: therefore, I dedicate it to His Magnificence Giuliano. Filippo da Casavecchia saw it, and he will be able to tell you more or less what it is like and the conversations I had with him, although I often enlarge and correct the text.

Magnificent Ambassador, you would like me to abandon this life and come and enjoy yours with you. I will do it anyway; but I am kept here by certain matters that I will have finalized within six weeks. What makes me hesitate is that those Soderinis are in Rome; while there, I would be obliged to visit and talk with them. I am afraid that upon my return, that I might not count on dismounting at home, but rather that I should dismount at Bargello as, although this state has solid foundations and great security, it is still new and, therefore, full of suspicion. There are plenty of 'know-it-all' like Pagolo Bertini who, in order to be impressive, would put others in prison and leave the troubles to me. I ask you to reassure me of this fear and then, come what may, I shall come and see you in any case at the time mentioned.

I discussed this little study of mine with Filippo and whether or not it would be a good idea to present it [to Giuliano], whether it was more convenient for me to take it myself or to send it to you. Against presenting it, would be my suspicion that he might not even read it and that that person, Ardinghelli, might take credit for this most recent of my endeavors. In favor of presenting it would be the necessity that hounds me, because I am in ruin and cannot continue on like this much longer without becoming despicable because of my poverty. Besides, there is my desire that these Medici gentlemen should begin to engage my services, even if they should start out by having me roll along a stone. Because if afterward I am unable to gain their favor, I would have only myself to blame. And when this study of mine was read, it would be evident that during the fifteen years that I spent studying the art of the state, I have neither slept nor fooled around, and anybody ought to be happy to use someone who has had so much experience at the expense of others. And my fidelity should not be doubted because, having always observed loyalty, I must not now learn how to break it. Whoever has been faithful and honest for forty-three years, as I have, is unable to change his nature; my poverty is a witness to my loyalty and honesty.

I would like you to tell me what your opinion is about all this. I recommend myself to you. Be happy.

Florence, December 10, 1513.
Niccolò Machiavelli

Niccolò Machiavelli, by Santi di Tito.

**DISCOVER OUR BOOKS
ACCESSING HERE!**